COOKIES
AND
CANDIES

Better Homes and Gardens

COOKIES
AND
CANDIES

MEREDITH PRESS
New York   Des Moines

CONTENTS

On our cover, a rustic chest brims with cookie and candy treasures. Sparkling Jewel Candies surround the base. Nestled inside are Gumdrop Gems, Coconut Diamonds, sugar-sprinkled Greek Cookies, red-coated Easy Sugarplums.

Perfect snack or fast dessert—cookies and candies with fruit or milk. Here we show Buttery Peanut Brittle, Salt Water Taffy, multicolored Bright-eyed Susans, frosted Stuffed Date Drops, and Lemon-drop Cookies. Just a sampling of many delicious recipes to come!

Better Homes and Gardens
TEST KITCHEN

Our checked seal assures you that every recipe in Cookies and Candies is tested and endorsed by the Better Homes and Gardens Test Kitchen. Each cookie and candy was tested till it measured up to high standards of family appeal, practicality, and downright deliciousness!

THE ABCs OF COOKIE MAKING

Happiness is a warm cookie; a full cookie jar when you come home from school or work; baking cookies for loved ones. After mastering a few cookie techniques, happiness will be the pride of serving perfect homemade cookies to family and friends. All of these recipes have been tested and retested in our Test Kitchen to develop the best balance of ingredients and standard methods. To insure success at home, measure all of the ingredients carefully and follow mixing directions to the letter.

For best results, make cookies with all-purpose flour that has been sifted before measuring. *Softened* butter or margarine creams best. A well creamed butter-sugar mixture will have a light, fluffy texture.

Shiny cookie sheets, 2 inches shorter and narrower than the oven, help cookies brown evenly. Baked cookies should be cooled on racks—this prevents sogginess. Use a cool sheet to bake remaining batches. Freeze refrigerator, drop, or bar cookie dough in freezer containers which have been properly sealed and labeled. Or put bar cookie dough in baking pan to freeze. Doughs will keep 6 to 12 months. Thaw only if necessary to spread, drop, or cut; bake as fresh cookies.

Party fare—in low jar, glazed
Lebkuchen and Springerle. Tiered jar
holds Spicy Hermits and Cherry
Refrigerator Cookies. Tall jar sports
gaily decorated Sugar Cookies.

Cookie types

DROP COOKIES

Characteristics: Dough is dropped by teaspoon onto cookie sheet. Added nuts or candies, as in Polka-dot Oatmeal Crisps, give a novelty texture to cookies.

Technique Pointers: Watch baking time carefully. Under-baking will cause a doughy product; overbaking tends to make cookies dry and hard with dark, crisp edges. Prevent excessive spreading of cookies by chilling the dough; dropping onto cold cookie sheet; baking at the correct temperature; and mounding dough when dropped.

Test for Doneness: Cookies should be delicately browned. The imprint of your finger will remain slightly visible when cookies are done.

REFRIGERATOR COOKIES

Characteristics: Dough is molded into rolls, wrapped, chilled thoroughly in the refrigerator, and then cut into thin slices for baking. Refrigerator cookies, such as Gumdrop Gems, are crisp and crunchy.

Technique Pointers: For uniform, thin slices mold dough into a smooth roll and chill thoroughly until it can be sliced easily. Cutting dough with a thin, sharp knife insures neat, trim edges and thin cookie slices (thick slices result in soft-textured cookie). Slice and bake cookies as needed. Re-wrap unused dough and store in the refrigerator for up to one week.

Test for Doneness: Cookies will be lightly browned.

MOLDED COOKIES

Characteristics: Dough is rolled into balls or thin pencil-shaped rolls between the hands. Some cookies, such as Peanut-butter Crinkles, are then flattened with the bottom of a glass which has been dipped in sugar or flour. Others are crisscrossed with the tines of a fork or pressed down with thumb before baking. Molded cookies are crisp and tender.

Technique Pointers: Molding cookies carefully produces a uniformly shaped cookie. Smooth surfaces insure even browning and desired texture.

Test for Doneness: Cookies should be lightly browned and set enough so that slight imprint remains when touched.

BAR COOKIES

Characteristics: A stiff dough that is spread or pressed evenly into a pan, baked, cooled, and cut in bars or diamonds. Bar cookies such as Chocolate Diamonds, have a thin delicate crust and rich, moist eating quality.

Technique Pointers: A hard crusty top will result from overmixing. Overbaking produces a dry, crumbly bar. Cool slightly before cutting to prevent crumbling.

Test for Doneness: Watch overbaking! Fudgy-type bars are done when a slight imprint remains after touching with finger and top has dull crust. Cake-like bars should be baked until a toothpick inserted in the center of the pan comes out clean.

ROLLED COOKIES

Characteristics: Dough is chilled, rolled out on board, and then cut in desired shapes with cutters or patterns. Some rolled cookies, such as Gingerbread Boys, are thin crisp cookies; others are thicker with a soft texture.

Technique Pointers: Use a lightly floured cookie cutter. Roll a small amount of dough at a time, keeping the rest chilled. Roll from center to edge as for pie crust. Thin dough makes crisper cookies. Excessive re-rolling and using too much flour on the board tends to make dry, tough cookies.

Test for Doneness: When done, cookies will be a delicate brown color. Time carefully to avoid overbaking.

PRESSED COOKIES

Characteristics: Dough is forced through a cookie press into desired shapes. Pressed cookies, such as Spritz, are very tender and crisp.

Technique Pointers: Keep dough pliable to obtain well-defined patterns on cookies. Chill dough slightly if it becomes too soft. Follow manufacturer's directions for using press. Cookies will retain better shape if pressed onto a cold cookie sheet. Bake cookies of like pattern on same cookie sheet; these cookies will then finish baking at the same time.

Test for Doneness: Pressed cookies are done when set with delicately browned edges.

Cookies in fine shape

Pastry cloth and stockinette covering for rolling pin make rolling cookies a snap! Start cutting at edge, work toward center. In a toot? Cut diamond-shaped cookies with pastry wheel using ruler as guideline—no rerolls!

Springerle rolling pin transfers pictures to dough like a cookie mold. Dust pin lightly with flour, then roll firmly across dough. Cut cookies apart with sharp knife. Another time use rolling pin with waffle or other fancy design.

Drop cookies are dropped from a teaspoon onto cookie sheet with the help of another teaspoon or rubber spatula. Mound dough to obtain more uniform shape. Space cookies about 2 inches apart—they spread a little while baking.

A cookie press makes gay shapes quick as a wink. Handle at top forces dough through desired form, the same as for a cake decorator. Just switch disks for other designs.

Molded cookies are rolled between hands into smooth 1-inch balls, then pressed down with tines of fork, either in one direction or crisscross. Others are flattened with floured glass.

Just for fun – decorate

Frost favorite cookies with Confectioners' Icing (see index) and decorate with nut halves, chopped nuts, a variety of candies, candied cherries or mixed fruits and peels, cake decorettes, or colored sugar.

Place cutter on cookie when icing is almost firm; sprinkle inside cutter with decorettes.

Sandwich two cookies together with icing; top with dollop of frosting and an animal cracker.

Decorating tube (a cone of waxed paper will do) and icing make names or frills atop cookie.

Store them right

Store soft cookies in a tightly covered jar; tuck in an apple wedge if they become dry. Keep crisp cookies in a jar with loose-fitting lid.

To freeze cookies, wrap in moisture-vaporproof material; place in sturdy container; overwrap with moisture-vaporproof material; seal, label, and freeze. Thaw, unopened, in the container.

EVERYDAY FAVORITES

THE ALL-AMERICAN CHOCOLATE CHIP

DARK RICH CHOCOLATE COOKIES

PRIZE BROWNIES

FLAVORFUL FRUIT COOKIES

SUGAR AND SPICE CLASSICS

OLD-FASHIONED CEREAL COOKIES

NUT-FLAVORED FAVORITES

Bake a variety of these wonderful
cookies: Robust Mincemeat Star Cookies,
Maple Nut Chews, frosted and unfrosted
Cocoa Drop Cookies. In the clear jar,
spot Oatmeal Chip Cookies. Below
are giant Paul Bunyan Sugar Cookies,
Caramel Chews, and Cake Brownies.

The all-American chocolate chip

CHOCOLATE CHIPPERS

½ cup shortening
½ cup granulated sugar
¼ cup brown sugar
1 egg
1 teaspoon vanilla
1 cup sifted all-purpose flour
½ teaspoon soda
¾ teaspoon salt
1 6-ounce package (1 cup) semisweet chocolate pieces
½ cup chopped California walnuts

Cream shortening, sugars, egg, and vanilla till fluffy. Sift together dry ingredients; stir into creamed mixture. Stir in chocolate and nuts. Drop from teaspoon 2 inches apart onto greased cookie sheet. Bake at 375° for 10 to 12 minutes. Remove from pan. Makes 3 dozen.

MOLASSES JUMBLES

Cream ⅔ cup shortening and ½ cup granulated sugar; add 1 egg and beat well. Sift together 2½ cups sifted all-purpose flour, 1 teaspoon soda, ¼ teaspoon salt, ½ teaspoon cinnamon, and dash ginger. Combine ½ cup light molasses and ½ cup buttermilk; add alternately with dry ingredients to creamed mixture. Stir in one 6-ounce package (1 cup) semisweet chocolate pieces. Drop from tablespoon 2 inches apart on ungreased cookie sheet. Bake at 350° for 12 to 15 minutes. Makes 72.

CHOCOLATE DIAMONDS

Cream ⅓ cup shortening, 1 cup brown sugar, and 1 teaspoon vanilla; add 1 egg and beat well. Sift together 1 cup sifted all-purpose flour, ¼ teaspoon soda, and ¼ teaspoon salt; add to creamed mixture; mix well. Stir in ½ to 1 cup semisweet chocolate pieces and ½ cup chopped California walnuts. Spread in greased 11x7x 1½-inch baking pan. Bake at 350° for 20 to 25 minutes. Cut in diamond shapes or bars while warm. Makes about 2 dozen.

Chocolate Chippers are a favorite cookie of all ages. First served at the Toll House Inn, this cookie has become a national classic.

OATMEAL CHIP COOKIES

Fancy version of an old favorite—

½ cup shortening
½ cup granulated sugar
½ cup brown sugar
½ teaspoon vanilla
1 egg
1 cup sifted all-purpose flour
½ teaspoon soda
½ teaspoon salt
1 cup quick-cooking rolled oats
1 6-ounce package (1 cup) semisweet
   chocolate pieces
½ cup chopped California walnuts

Thoroughly cream shortening, sugars, and vanilla. Beat in egg, then 1 tablespoon water. Sift together flour, soda, and salt; add to creamed mixture, blending well. Stir in the rolled oats, chocolate, and walnuts. Drop by rounded teaspoons onto a greased cookie sheet about 2 inches apart. Bake at 375° for 10 to 12 minutes. Cool slightly before removing from pan. Makes 3½ to 4 dozen.
Note: For *Polka-dot Oatmeal Crisps*, substitute one 10½-ounce package candy-coated chocolate pieces for chocolate chips and nuts.

BUSY-BEE CHIPPERS

½ cup butter or margarine
⅓ cup brown sugar
⅓ cup honey
1 egg
½ teaspoon vanilla
1 cup plus 2 tablespoons sifted
   all-purpose flour
½ teaspoon soda
½ teaspoon salt
1 6-ounce package (1 cup) semisweet
   chocolate pieces
½ cup chopped California walnuts

Cream butter; add sugar and honey, mixing well. Add egg and vanilla; beat well. Sift together flour, soda, and salt; add to creamed mixture, mixing well.

Stir in chocolate pieces and nuts. Drop batter from teaspoon onto ungreased cookie sheet. Bake in moderate oven (375°) for 10 to 12 minutes. Makes about 4 dozen cookies.

Dark rich chocolate cookies

BROWNIE MERINGUES

2 egg whites
Dash salt
½ teaspoon vinegar
½ teaspoon vanilla
½ cup granulated sugar
1 6-ounce package (1 cup) semisweet chocolate pieces, melted and
   cooled
¾ cup chopped California walnuts

Beat egg whites with salt, vinegar, and vanilla till soft peaks form. Gradually add sugar,
beating to stiff peaks. Fold in chocolate and
nuts. Drop from teaspoon onto greased cookie
sheet. Bake in moderate oven (350°) about 10
minutes. Makes about 3 dozen cookies.

Mocha Frosted Drops hold that rich chocolate
flavor you sometimes crave. Squares of pure
chocolate, brown sugar, and buttermilk start
this cookie on the good-eating road. Then added

CHOCO-SCOTCH BARS

½ cup butter or margarine
1 cup granulated sugar
2 eggs
1½ teaspoons vanilla
1 cup sifted all-purpose flour
¼ teaspoon salt
1½ ounces unsweetened chocolate,
   melted
½ cup chopped pecans

Cream butter and sugar till fluffy; add eggs
and vanilla; beat well. Add flour and salt.
Divide batter in half. Add chocolate to half;
spread in greased 8x8x2-inch pan. Stir nuts
into remaining batter; spread over chocolate
layer. Bake at 350° for 30 minutes. Makes 24.

chocolate pieces and nuts make for double
chocolate flavor. A creamy topping of Mocha
Frosting brings on still more chocolate, but
this time adds a flavor suggestion of coffee.

MOCHA FROSTED DROPS

- ½ cup shortening
- 2 1-ounce squares unsweetened chocolate
- 1 cup brown sugar
- 1 egg
- 1 teaspoon vanilla
- ½ cup buttermilk *or* sour milk
- 1½ cups sifted all-purpose flour
- ½ teaspoon baking powder
- ½ teaspoon soda
- ¼ teaspoon salt
- ½ cup chopped California walnuts
- 1 6-ounce package (1 cup) semi-sweet chocolate pieces

Melt shortening and unsweetened chocolate together in a saucepan. Cool 10 minutes. Stir in the brown sugar. Beat in the egg, vanilla, and buttermilk or sour milk.

Sift together dry ingredients and add to chocolate mixture. Stir in nuts and chocolate pieces. Drop from teaspoon on greased cookie sheet. Bake at 375° about 10 minutes. Remove from pan and cool. Frost with Mocha Frosting. Makes about 3½ dozen cookies.

Mocha Frosting: Cream together ¼ cup butter, 2 tablespoons cocoa (regular-type, dry), 2 teaspoons instant coffee powder, and dash salt. Beat in 2½ cups sifted confectioners' sugar, 1½ teaspoons vanilla, and enough milk (about 3 tablespoons) for spreading consistency.

MALTED OATMEAL BARS

- ½ cup butter or margarine
- 1 cup granulated sugar
- 2 eggs
- 1 teaspoon vanilla
- ½ cup sifted all-purpose flour
- ¼ teaspoon salt
- ½ cup chocolate-flavored malted-milk powder
- ¾ cup quick-cooking rolled oats
- ½ cup chopped California walnuts

Cream butter and sugar. Add eggs and vanilla. Beat well. Sift together flour, salt, and malted-milk powder. Add to creamed mixture; mix well. Stir in oats and nuts. Spread in greased 9x9x2-inch baking pan. Bake at 350° for 35 minutes. Cool. Cut in bars. Makes 2 dozen.

FUDGE NUGGETS

Great for milk and cookie fans—

- ¾ cup shortening
- 1 cup granulated sugar
- 1 egg
- 1 teaspoon vanilla
- 2 1-ounce squares unsweetened chocolate, melted and slightly cooled
- 1½ cups sifted all-purpose flour
- ½ teaspoon salt
- 1½ teaspoons instant coffee powder
- ¾ cup milk
- 1 cup quick-cooking rolled oats
- ½ cup chopped nuts

Cream shortening and sugar till fluffy; beat in egg and vanilla. Stir in chocolate. Sift together flour, salt, and instant coffee powder. Add to chocolate mixture alternately with milk. Stir in rolled oats and nuts.

Drop mixture from teaspoon on ungreased cookie sheet. Bake in a moderate oven (350°) 12 to 15 minutes or till done. Dust with confectioners' sugar. Makes about 4 dozen cookies.

COCOA DROP COOKIES

- 1 cup butter or margarine
- 1¾ cups granulated sugar
- 1 cup cottage cheese
- 1 teaspoon vanilla
- 2 eggs

. . .

- 2½ cups sifted all-purpose flour
- ½ cup cocoa (regular-type, dry)
- 1 teaspoon soda
- 1 teaspoon baking powder
- ½ teaspoon salt

Cream butter and sugar till fluffy; add cottage cheese and vanilla and beat thoroughly. Add eggs, one at a time, beating well after each addition. Sift together flour, cocoa, soda, baking powder, and salt; gradually add to creamed mixture. Drop by rounded teaspoons onto greased cookie sheet. Bake at 350° about 12 minutes. Let stand a few minutes before removing from cookie sheet. When cool, frost with Confectioners' Icing (see index), if desired. Makes about 6½ dozen cookies.

Prize brownies

FUDGE BROWNIES

½ cup butter or margarine
1 cup granulated sugar
1 teaspoon vanilla
2 eggs
2 1-ounce squares unsweetened
chocolate, melted
½ cup sifted all-purpose flour
½ cup chopped California walnuts

Cream first 3 ingredients. Add eggs; beat well. Blend in chocolate, then stir in flour and nuts. Bake in greased 8x8x2-inch pan at 325° for 30 to 35 minutes. Cool. Frost with Fudge Frosting and top with nut halves, or sift confectioners' sugar over top, or frost with pink Confectioners' Icing (see index) and decorate with mints. Cut in squares or diamonds.

Fudge Frosting: Melt ½ of a 1-ounce square unsweetened chocolate with 1 tablespoon butter or margarine and 2 tablespoons milk over *very low heat;* stir constantly. Beat in ¾ cup sifted confectioners' sugar.

PEANUT BUTTER BARS

½ cup peanut butter
¼ cup butter or margarine
1 teaspoon vanilla
1 cup brown sugar
2 eggs
⅔ cup sifted all-purpose flour
¾ cup chopped salted peanuts

Cream first 4 ingredients. Add eggs, one at a time; beat well. Stir in flour and peanuts. Spread mixture evenly in a greased 8x8x2-inch pan. Bake at 350° for 25 to 30 minutes. Cool slightly before cutting. Cut in bars. Remove from pan; cool. Sift confectioners' sugar over tops. Makes about 2½ dozen bars.

Top or frost them any way you like—these rich, moist, and chewy Fudge Brownies will be favorites with all ages—

CAKE BROWNIES

If you take a fancy to cake-like cookies, these brownies will be a favorite of yours—

¼ cup butter or margarine
1 cup granulated sugar
2 egg yolks
¼ cup milk
½ teaspoon vanilla
2 1-ounce squares unsweetened chocolate, melted and cooled

. . .

⅔ cup sifted all-purpose flour
½ teaspoon baking powder
½ teaspoon salt
⅓ cup chopped nuts
2 stiff-beaten egg whites

Cream butter and sugar till fluffy. Add egg yolks, milk, and vanilla; beat well. Stir in melted chocolate. Sift together dry ingredients; add to creamed mixture and mix well. Stir in chopped nuts. Fold in egg whites. Turn into greased and floured 9x9x2-inch baking pan. Bake at 350° for 25 to 30 minutes. Cool. Sprinkle top with sifted confectioners' sugar. Makes about 16 brownies.

MAPLE NUT CHEWS

⅓ cup butter or margarine
½ cup brown sugar
½ teaspoon maple flavoring
1 egg
½ cup sifted all-purpose flour
¼ teaspoon salt
¼ teaspoon baking powder
½ cup raisins
½ cup chopped California walnuts

In a saucepan, melt butter and sugar; cool slightly. Beat in maple flavoring and egg. Sift flour with salt and baking powder; stir into butter mixture. Stir in raisins and walnuts; spread in greased 8x8x2-inch pan. Bake in moderate oven (350°) for 25 to 30 minutes. Cool slightly; cut in bars. Makes 16 bars.

CHOCOLATE PEANUT BARS

¼ cup butter or margarine
2 1-ounce squares unsweetened
  chocolate
1 cup granulated sugar
¼ cup crunchy peanut butter
2 eggs
½ cup sifted all-purpose flour
¼ teaspoon salt
½ teaspoon vanilla

Melt butter and chocolate; cool. Blend in sugar and peanut butter. Beat in eggs one at a time. Add remaining ingredients; beat till smooth. Pour into greased 8x8x2-inch pan and bake at 350° for 25 minutes. Cut in bars.

MARBLE BROWNIES

Cream ½ cup butter or margarine, ¾ cup granulated sugar, and 1½ teaspoons vanilla. Add 2 eggs; beat till blended. Sift together ⅔ cup sifted all-purpose flour, ½ teaspoon baking powder, and ¼ teaspoon salt. Stir into creamed mixture. Place *half* of batter in another bowl; blend in one 1-ounce square unsweetened chocolate, melted. Marble batters in greased 8x8x2-inch pan, following photo directions. Bake at 350° for 30 minutes; cool. Makes about 16.

CHIPPER DATE BROWNIES

These light cake-type brownies boast a crunchy baked-on topping—

1 8-ounce package (1½ cups) pitted
  dates, chopped
1 cup boiling water
1 cup shortening
1 cup granulated sugar
2 eggs
1 teaspoon vanilla
• • •
1¾ cups sifted all-purpose flour
¼ cup cocoa (regular-type, dry)
½ teaspoon soda
½ teaspoon salt
½ to 1 cup broken California
  walnuts
1 6-ounce package (1 cup) semisweet chocolate pieces

Combine chopped dates and boiling water; cool to room temperature. Thoroughly cream shortening, sugar, eggs, and vanilla; stir in date mixture. Sift together dry ingredients; add to creamed mixture. Turn into greased 15½x10½ x1-inch jellyroll pan. Sprinkle nuts and chocolate pieces evenly over top. Bake in a moderate oven (375°) for 25 to 30 minutes or till done. Cool. Cut in squares.

To marble the two batters for Marble Brownies, drop chocolate batter by teaspoons checkerboard fashion. Fill empty spaces with light batter.

For the swirls that make the Marble Brownies so attractive, zigzag rubber spatula or scraper through the two batters lightly, being careful not to blend them too well. Top cooled brownies with a chocolate frosting.

MIDNIGHT BROWNIES

1½ cups semisweet chocolate
   pieces (about 9 ounces)
6 tablespoons butter or margarine
2 beaten eggs
⅓ cup honey
1 teaspoon vanilla
½ cup sifted all-purpose flour
½ teaspoon baking powder
½ cup chopped Brazil nuts

Melt semisweet chocolate pieces and butter together in a small saucepan over low heat, stirring constantly; cool.

Gradually add honey to beaten eggs. Blend in chocolate mixture and vanilla. Sift together flour and baking powder; add to chocolate mixture. Then mix in the nuts. Turn into a greased 9x9x2-inch pan. Bake in a moderate oven (350°) for about 25 minutes. Cool and cut into squares or bars. Makes about 1½ dozen bars.

CHOCOLATE MALT BARS

½ cup shortening
¾ cup granulated sugar
½ teaspoon vanilla
2 eggs
1 1-ounce square unsweetened
   chocolate, melted and cooled
1 cup sifted all-purpose flour
½ cup chocolate-flavored malted-
   milk powder
½ teaspoon baking powder
½ teaspoon salt
½ cup chopped California walnuts
Malt Frosting

Cream together the shortening, sugar, and vanilla till fluffy; beat in the eggs. Blend in melted and cooled chocolate. Sift together dry ingredients; stir into creamed mixture. Fold in chopped nuts. Spread in greased 8x8x2-inch baking pan. Bake in moderate oven (350°) for 20 to 25 minutes; cool. Frost with Malt Frosting and cut in 2x1-inch bars. Makes 2½ dozen.

Malt Frosting: Cream 2 tablespoons softened butter or margarine, ¼ cup chocolate-flavored malted-milk powder, and dash salt. Slowly beat in 1 cup sifted confectioners' sugar and enough light cream to make of spreading consistency (about 1½ tablespoons).

PINEAPPLE-CHOCOLATE SQUARES

¾ cup shortening
1½ cups granulated sugar
1 teaspoon vanilla
3 eggs
1 cup sifted all-purpose flour
1 teaspoon baking powder
½ teaspoon salt
½ teaspoon cinnamon
¼ cup chopped pecans
2 1-ounce squares unsweetened
   chocolate, melted and cooled
1 8¾-ounce can (1 cup) crushed
   pineapple, well drained

Cream shortening, sugar, and vanilla till fluffy; beat in eggs. Sift together flour, baking powder, salt, and cinnamon; stir into creamed mixture. Divide batter; to one half add nuts and chocolate. Spread in greased 9x9x2-inch baking pan. Add pineapple to remaining batter; spread *carefully* over chocolate layer. Bake in a moderate oven (350°) about 35 minutes or till done. Sprinkle with confectioners' sugar, if desired. Cut in squares or bars.

BUTTERSCOTCH BROWNIES

¼ cup butter or margarine
1 cup brown sugar
1 egg
½ teaspoon vanilla
¾ cup sifted all-purpose flour
½ teaspoon salt
¼ teaspoon nutmeg
1 egg white
1 tablespoon light corn syrup
½ cup granulated sugar
½ cup chopped California walnuts

In saucepan combine butter and brown sugar; cook over low heat till mixture bubbles; stir constantly. Cool slightly. Beat in egg and vanilla. Sift together dry ingredients. Stir into sugar mixture. Spread in greased 8x8x2-inch pan.

Beat egg white to soft peaks; gradually add corn syrup, then sugar, a small amount at a time, beating till *very stiff peaks* form. Fold in chopped nuts. Spread over dough. Bake at 350° for 25 to 30 minutes. Cool; cut in 2-inch squares. Makes 16 squares.

Flavorful fruit cookies

LEMON TEA CAKES

1½ teaspoons vinegar
½ cup milk
½ cup butter or margarine
¾ cup granulated sugar
1 egg
1 teaspoon shredded lemon peel
1¾ cups sifted all-purpose flour
1 teaspoon baking powder
¼ teaspoon *each* soda and salt
Lemon Glaze

Stir vinegar into milk. Cream butter and sugar till fluffy. Beat in egg and peel. Sift together dry ingredients; add to creamed mixture alternately with milk, beating after each addition. Drop from teaspoon 2 inches apart on ungreased cookie sheet. Bake at 350° for 12 to 14 minutes. Remove at once from sheet; brush tops with *Lemon Glaze:* Mix ¾ cup granulated sugar and ¼ cup lemon juice. If desired, garnish with tinted coconut. Makes 4 dozen.

APPLE-ORANGE BROWNIES

Combine 6 tablespoons butter or margarine and 1 cup brown sugar in saucepan; cook and stir till melted. Beat in ½ cup applesauce, 1 teaspoon shredded orange peel, 1 beaten egg, and 1 teaspoon vanilla. Sift together 1¼ cups sifted all-purpose flour, 1 teaspoon baking powder, ½ teaspoon salt, and ¼ teaspoon soda. Stir into mixture in saucepan. Stir in ½ cup chopped California walnuts.

Spread in greased 15½x10½x1-inch pan. Bake at 350° for 15 minutes. While warm, top with *Orange Glaze:* Combine 1½ cups sifted confectioners' sugar, ½ teaspoon vanilla, dash salt, and about 2 tablespoons orange juice.

A refreshing treat for any occasion—fruit cookies and ice cold punch. Take your choice from tangy Lemon Tea Cakes with coconut bonnets, moist Apple-orange Brownies, and fancy Date-marmalade Pastries.

MINCEMEAT STAR COOKIES

1⅓ cups shortening
1½ cups granulated sugar
2 eggs
1 teaspoon vanilla
1 teaspoon grated orange peel
4 cups sifted all-purpose flour
3 teaspoons baking powder
½ teaspoon salt
2 to 3 tablespoons milk
Mincemeat Filling

Thoroughly cream shortening, sugar, eggs, and vanilla. Stir in peel. Sift together dry ingredients; add to creamed mixture alternately with milk. Divide dough in half; chill. On lightly floured surface, roll each half to ⅛ inch. Cut with 2¾-inch round cutter. Cut small star in centers of *half* the cookies. Place 1 heaping teaspoon filling on each plain cookie. Top with a cutout cookie; press edges with fork to seal. Bake on greased cookie sheet at 375° for 12 minutes. Makes 2½ dozen.

Mincemeat Filling: Break one 9-ounce package mincemeat in pieces. Add 2 tablespoons granulated sugar, 2 teaspoons grated orange peel, 1 teaspoon grated lemon peel, ½ cup orange juice, and ¼ cup lemon juice. Heat, stirring till lumps are broken; simmer 1 minute. Cool; stir in ¼ cup chopped California walnuts.

DATE-MARMALADE PASTRIES

1 10-ounce package pie crust mix
1 3-ounce package cream cheese
1 tablespoon milk
1 pound pitted dates
1 cup orange marmalade

Blend pie crust mix, cream cheese, and milk. Divide dough in half. Roll each part to 10x12-inch rectangle on lightly floured surface. Cut with pastry wheel in 2-inch squares. Stuff dates with marmalade. Place date in center of each square and bring diagonal corners to center; seal. Bake at 400° for 10 minutes or till lightly browned. Makes 5 dozen.

These rich Pineapple Drop Cookies are delicately flavored with pineapple preserves, making them a perfect go-together with ice cream or hot tea. They're chewy in the center, yet crisp around the edges. Be sure to frost cookies just before serving—makes them easier to store.

PINEAPPLE DROP COOKIES

3/4 cup butter or margarine,
   softened
1 cup granulated sugar
1 egg
1/4 cup pineapple preserves
2 1/4 cups sifted all-purpose flour
1 teaspoon soda
1/2 teaspoon salt

Cream butter and sugar till light. Beat in egg and preserves. Sift together dry ingredients; add, mixing thoroughly. Drop from teaspoon, 2 inches apart, on ungreased cookie sheet. Bake at 375° for 10 minutes. Cool 1 or 2 minutes; remove from pan. Top with preserves and a walnut half just before serving. Makes 42.

MARMALADE FIG BARS

1 1/2 cups sifted all-purpose flour
1 teaspoon baking powder
1/2 teaspoon salt
1 1/2 cups quick-cooking rolled oats
1 cup brown sugar
3/4 cup butter or margarine
1 cup chopped dried figs
1 cup orange marmalade

Sift first 3 ingredients together. Add oats and brown sugar. With pastry blender, cut in butter till crumbly. Stir in figs. Pat 2/3 of mixture into 13x9x2-inch pan. Spread with marmalade. Sprinkle remaining mixture over top. Bake at 375° for 30 to 35 minutes. Cool; cut into bars. Makes about 2 dozen cookies.

FRUIT COCKTAIL GEMS

1 1-pound can (2 cups) fruit
   cocktail
½ cup butter or margarine
½ cup brown sugar
¼ cup granulated sugar
½ teaspoon vanilla
1 egg

. . .

2 cups sifted all-purpose flour
½ teaspoon baking powder
½ teaspoon soda
½ teaspoon salt
½ teaspoon cinnamon
¼ teaspoon cloves
½ cup chopped California walnuts
½ cup raisins

Drain fruit cocktail, reserving syrup. Cream next four ingredients till fluffy. Add egg; beat well. Sift together dry ingredients; add alternately to creamed mixture with ⅓ cup of the reserved fruit cocktail syrup. Stir in chopped nuts, raisins, and fruit cocktail. Drop from teaspoon onto greased cookie sheet. Bake in a moderate oven (375°) for 10 to 12 minutes. Cool. Makes about 3½ dozen cookies.

CHERRY REFRIGERATOR COOKIES

¾ cup butter or margarine
½ cup granulated sugar
½ cup brown sugar
2 eggs
2¾ cups sifted all-purpose flour
1 teaspoon baking powder
¼ teaspoon salt
¼ teaspoon soda
½ teaspoon cinnamon
1 cup chopped candied cherries
1 cup chopped California walnuts

Cream butter and sugars together till fluffy; add eggs and beat well. Sift dry ingredients together and stir into creamed mixture. Add cherries and nuts. Shape into rolls about 1½ inches in diameter. Wrap in waxed paper or foil and chill overnight. Slice ¼ inch thick. Place on greased cookie sheet 1 inch apart. Bake at 375° for 8 to 10 minutes, or till delicately browned. Makes 8 dozen cookies.

LUNCH-BOX DATE SQUARES

For dessert, cut larger squares and top with vanilla ice cream—

3 eggs
1 cup granulated sugar
1 cup packaged biscuit mix
½ teaspoon salt
1 8-ounce package pitted dates,
   cut up (1½ cups)
½ cup chopped California walnuts

Beat eggs till light; add sugar gradually, beating until thick and lemon-colored. Combine biscuit mix and salt; stir into egg mixture. Add dates and nuts; mix well. Pour into greased 9x9x2-inch baking pan. Bake in a moderate oven (350°) for 30 to 35 minutes. Cool slightly; cut in 2-inch squares. Makes 16 squares.

OLD-FASHIONED RAISIN BARS

A cake-type cookie—tender, moist and spicy! For an after-school snack, serve with mugs of milk—

1 cup raisins
1 cup water
½ cup shortening or salad oil

. . .

1 cup granulated sugar
1 slightly beaten egg
1¾ cups sifted all-purpose
   flour
¼ teaspoon salt
1 teaspoon soda
1 teaspoon cinnamon
½ teaspoon nutmeg
½ teaspoon allspice
¼ teaspoon cloves

. . .

½ cup chopped California walnuts

Combine raisins and water in a saucepan; bring to boiling; remove from heat. Stir in shortening; cool to lukewarm.

Stir in sugar and egg. Sift together dry ingredients; beat into raisin mixture. Stir in nuts. Pour into greased 15½x10½x1-inch baking pan. Bake in moderate oven (375°) for 12 minutes or till done. When cool, cut in bars. Dust lightly with confectioners' sugar, or frost while warm. Makes about 4 dozen bars.

Sugar and spice classics

CRISP GINGER COOKIES

¾ cup brown sugar
¼ cup butter or margarine, melted
1 egg

. . .

¾ cup sifted all-purpose flour
1 teaspoon baking powder
¼ teaspoon salt
2 tablespoons finely snipped
   candied ginger

Combine brown sugar and butter; beat in egg. Sift together flour, baking powder, and salt; stir into sugar mixture. Baking only 6 or 7 cookies at one time, drop dough from teaspoon, 2 inches apart, onto greased cookie sheet. Sprinkle a few pieces of ginger on top of each. Bake at 325° for 10 to 12 minutes or till lightly browned. Let cool on sheet *only half a minute*, then *quickly* remove to cooling rack. (If last few cookies do stick, return pan to oven briefly to reheat.) Makes about 3 dozen cookies.

GINGERSNAPS

Crinkle-topped and spicy—

¾ cup shortening
1 cup brown sugar
¼ cup molasses
1 egg
2¼ cups sifted all-purpose flour
2 teaspoons soda
½ teaspoon salt
1 teaspoon ginger
1 teaspoon cinnamon
½ teaspoon cloves

Cream together shortening, brown sugar, molasses, and egg till light and fluffy. Sift together dry ingredients; stir into molasses mixture till blended. Form in small balls. Roll in granulated sugar and place 2 inches apart on greased cookie sheet. Bake at 375° about 10 minutes. Remove from pan immediately. Makes about 5 dozen cookies.

Crisp Ginger Cookies make the perfect flavor complement for orange sherbet. They're golden-edged, fragile, and sugary crisp—just right for a snack. Snips of candied ginger add a delightful Oriental touch. Try these cookies with hot tea too.

SPICY HERMITS

1/2 cup shortening
1 cup brown sugar
1 egg
2 tablespoons water
1 1/2 cups sifted all-purpose flour
1 tablespoon instant coffee powder
1/2 teaspoon soda
1/2 teaspoon cinnamon
1/4 teaspoon salt
1/4 teaspoon nutmeg
1/4 teaspoon cloves
3/4 cup raisins
1/2 cup broken California walnuts

Thoroughly cream shortening and brown sugar. Add egg; beat well. Stir in water. Sift together dry ingredients; add to creamed mixture. Stir in raisins and nuts. Drop from teaspoon 2 inches apart on lightly greased cookie sheet. Bake in a moderate oven (375°) for 10 minutes. Makes about 3 1/2 dozen cookies.

LEMON MACE ROUNDS

2 cups sifted all-purpose flour
2 teaspoons baking powder
1/2 teaspoon salt
1/4 teaspoon mace
. . .
2 eggs
2/3 cup salad oil
3/4 cup granulated sugar
1/4 cup brown sugar
2 teaspoons lemon juice
2 teaspoons grated lemon peel
. . .
1/4 cup granulated sugar
1/2 teaspoon nutmeg
1/4 teaspoon mace

Sift flour, baking powder, salt, and 1/4 teaspoon mace together. Combine next 6 ingredients; beat until thick. Stir in dry ingredients. Drop by teaspoon about 2 inches apart on lightly greased cookie sheet.

Combine 1/4 cup granulated sugar, nutmeg, and 1/4 teaspoon mace. Lightly butter bottom of glass; dip in sugar and spice mixture and press cookies flat. Bake in hot oven (400°) for about 8 minutes or until lightly browned. Makes about 3 dozen cookies.

JOE FROGGERS

4 cups sifted all-purpose flour
1 1/2 teaspoons salt
1 1/2 teaspoons ginger
1/2 teaspoon cloves
1/2 teaspoon nutmeg
1/4 teaspoon allspice
. . .
1/3 cup water
1/2 teaspoon rum flavoring
1 teaspoon soda
1 cup dark molasses
1/2 cup shortening
1 cup granulated sugar

Sift together the flour, salt, ginger, cloves, nutmeg, and allspice. Combine water and rum flavoring. Add soda to molasses. Thoroughly cream shortening and sugar. Add *half* the dry ingredients, *half* the water and rum flavoring, then *half* the molasses, blending well after each addition. Repeat. Chill dough for several hours or overnight.

On well-floured surface, roll 1/4 inch thick and cut with a 3-inch cutter. Bake on a greased cookie sheet in a moderate oven (375°) for 10 to 12 minutes or until lightly browned; watch carefully so they do not burn. Let stand a few minutes; then remove. Makes about 3 dozen.

CARAWAY COOKIES

1 cup butter or margarine
1 cup granulated sugar
2 beaten eggs
2 3/4 cups sifted all-purpose flour
1 teaspoon soda
1/2 teaspoon cream of tartar
Dash salt
1/2 cup chopped mixed candied fruits
    and peels
1/2 cup light raisins
2 tablespoons caraway seed
2 tablespoons rosewater *or* water

Cream butter, sugar, and eggs till fluffy. Sift together flour, soda, cream of tartar, and salt; add to creamed mixture. Stir in remaining ingredients. Drop from teaspoon onto ungreased cookie sheet. Flatten with glass dipped in flour; center each with a light raisin. Bake at 375° for 8 to 10 minutes. Cool on rack. Makes 4 1/2 dozen.

DARK HERB COOKIES

½ cup shortening
½ cup granulated sugar
1 egg
½ cup molasses
2¼ cups sifted all-purpose flour
2 teaspoons soda
3 teaspoons ginger
1 teaspoon cinnamon
½ teaspoon cloves
¼ teaspoon salt
⅓ cup hot strong coffee
2 tablespoons anise seed
2 teaspoons coriander seed,
   crushed

Cream together shortening and sugar; beat in egg. Stir in molasses. Sift together flour, soda, ginger, cinnamon, cloves, and salt. Add alternately to creamed mixture with coffee, mixing thoroughly. Stir in anise and coriander seed. Drop from teaspoon onto greased cookie sheet, 2 inches apart. Bake in a moderate oven (350°) for 8 to 10 minutes. Cool on rack.

Frost with *Vanilla Glaze:* Combine 2 cups sifted confectioners' sugar, 1 teaspoon vanilla, and enough milk to make spreading consistency. Top each cookie with California Walnut half. Makes about 3½ dozen cookies.

Just by their fragrance, Dark Herb Cookies reveal rich spicy flavor. A smooth glaze and crisp walnut halves make them extra pretty.

GUMDROP GEMS

Buttery rich refrigerator cookies—

1 cup butter or margarine
1½ cups sifted confectioners'
   sugar
1 teaspoon vanilla
1 egg
   . . .
2½ cups sifted all-purpose flour
1 teaspoon soda
1 teaspoon cream of tartar
¼ teaspoon salt
1 cup small gumdrops, sliced*

Thoroughly cream the butter, confectioners' sugar, and vanilla; beat in egg. Sift together flour, soda, cream of tartar, and salt; gradually stir into creamed mixture; mix well.

Shape dough into roll 2 inches in diameter and 12 inches long. Wrap in waxed paper; chill several hours or overnight.

Cut ¼-inch-thick slices. Place on ungreased cookie sheet. Decorate tops with gumdrop slices. Bake in a moderate oven (375°) about 12 minutes or till lightly browned. Cool slightly before removing from pan. Makes about 4 dozen cookies.

*Remove black candies.

CARDAMOM COOKIES

1 cup sifted all-purpose flour
½ cup granulated sugar
⅛ to ¼ teaspoon ground cardamom
Dash cinnamon
¼ teaspoon shredded lemon peel
¼ cup ground almonds
6 tablespoons butter or margarine
1 beaten egg
2 teaspoons milk
Granulated sugar

Sift together flour, sugar, and spices; stir in peel and almonds. Cut in butter till mixture resembles coarse crumbs. Stir in egg and milk till mixture forms a ball; chill.

Roll out to about ⅛-inch thickness. Cut into circles 1¾ inches in diameter. Place on ungreased cookie sheet; sprinkle with sugar. Bake in a hot oven (400°) for 6 to 8 minutes or till edges are brown. Makes about 7 dozen.

PAUL BUNYAN SUGAR COOKIES

1½ cups butter or margarine
1½ cups granulated sugar
2 eggs
1 tablespoon vanilla
2 tablespoons milk
½ cup raisins
4 cups sifted all-purpose flour
3 teaspoons baking powder
½ teaspoon salt

Cream together shortening, sugar, eggs, and vanilla till light and fluffy. Stir in milk and raisins. Sift together flour, baking powder, and salt; stir into creamed mixture, blending well. Chill 1 hour.

On lightly floured surface, roll chilled dough to ¼-inch thickness. Cut with 2-pound coffee can or lid of round canister (about 5 inches in diameter). Sprinkle tops of cookies with granulated sugar. Place cookies about 1 inch apart on ungreased cookie sheet. Bake in moderate oven (375°) for 10 minutes or till cookies are lightly browned. Remove from pan with wide spatula. Makes 14 large cookies.

VANILLA WAFERS

½ cup butter or margarine
½ cup shortening
⅔ cup granulated sugar
2 teaspoons vanilla
1 teaspoon salt
2 eggs
2¾ cups sifted all-purpose
   flour

Cream butter, shortening, and sugar. Add vanilla and salt. Add eggs, one at a time, beating well after each. Stir in sifted flour, mixing well. Drop from a teaspoon 2 inches apart on greased cookie sheet. Flatten with floured, flat-bottom glass. Bake in moderate oven (375°) for 8 to 10 minutes or till delicately browned on edges. Remove immediately from pan. Makes 7 to 8 dozen cookies.

Orange-glazed Wafers: If desired, while cookies are hot, brush with mixture of ½ cup sifted confectioners' sugar, 1 tablespoon orange juice, and ¼ teaspoon grated orange peel. Dot with bits of candied ginger.

Italians serve their famous gelati (ice cream) with a flourish of Sugar-cookie Fans! Each dish rates one or two thin cookies poked in ice cream scoops at a jaunty angle.

SUGAR-COOKIE FANS

Cream together ⅔ cup shortening, ¾ cup granulated sugar, 1 egg, ½ teaspoon grated orange peel, and ½ teaspoon vanilla till fluffy. Stir in 4 teaspoons milk. Sift together 2 cups sifted all-purpose flour, 1½ teaspoons baking powder, and ¼ teaspoon salt; stir into creamed mixture, blending well. Divide dough in half; chill 1 hour. On lightly floured surface, roll to ⅛ inch. Cut around a canister lid or plate to make 8-inch circles. (For scalloped-edged fans, cut with a pastry wheel.) Then cut each circle, like a pie, into 8 wedges. With back of knife or edge of spatula, mark each cookie with lines that radiate from center to outside. Sprinkle with granulated sugar. Place 1 inch apart on lightly greased cookie sheet. Bake at 375° for 6 to 7 minutes. Cool slightly; remove from pan. Makes 3 dozen.

Old-fashioned cereal cookies

CEREAL-PEANUT BARS

Tastes almost like a candy bar—

- ½ cup light corn syrup
- ¼ cup brown sugar
- Dash salt
- 1 cup peanut butter
- 1 teaspoon vanilla
- 2 cups crisp rice cereal
- 1 cup corn flakes, slightly crushed
- 1 6-ounce package (1 cup) semisweet chocolate pieces

Combine syrup, sugar, and salt in saucepan; bring to a full boil. Stir in peanut butter. Remove from heat. Stir in vanilla, cereals, and chocolate pieces. Press into a buttered 9x9x2-inch pan. Chill 1 hour. Cut in small bars or squares. (For easy serving, store in refrigerator.) Makes about 2 dozen pieces.

MAPLE PRALINE COOKIES

- ⅔ cup shortening
- ⅔ cup brown sugar
- 1 egg
- ¼ cup milk
- ½ teaspoon maple flavoring
- 1¾ cups sifted all-purpose flour
- ¼ teaspoon salt
- ¼ teaspoon soda
- 2 cups crisp rice cereal

Cream shortening and sugar till fluffy. Beat in egg, milk, and flavoring. Sift together flour, salt, and soda; add to creamed mixture; mix well. Stir in cereal. Drop from teaspoon 2 inches apart on greased cookie sheet. Flatten with bottom of glass. Bake at 375° for 8 to 10 minutes. Makes about 3 dozen cookies.

Chewy with oatmeal, yet buttery rich. Scotch Teas are the type of cookie you can't stop eating. Good thing they're a snap to make.

APPLE-FILLED OATMEAL COOKIES

Apple Filling: In saucepan combine 1 cup finely diced unpared apple, ¼ cup raisins, ¼ cup chopped pecans, ½ cup granulated sugar, and 2 tablespoons water. Cook and stir till thick and apple is tender, about 10 minutes.

Oatmeal Cookies: Cream 1 cup butter or margarine and 1 cup brown sugar till fluffy. Beat in 2 eggs. Sift together 2 cups sifted all-purpose flour, 2 teaspoons baking powder, ½ teaspoon salt, 1 teaspoon cinnamon, and ½ teaspoon cloves; add to creamed mixture alternately with ½ cup milk. Stir in 2 cups quick-cooking rolled oats.

Set aside about ¾ cup of the dough. Drop remainder from teaspoon onto greased cookie sheet. Make small depression in center of each cookie; top with Apple Filling and small amount of reserved dough. Bake at 375° for 10 to 12 minutes. Makes about 3 dozen cookies.

BUTTERSCOTCH BARS

Combine 6 tablespoons butter or margarine, melted, ½ cup malted cereal nuggets, 1 cup brown sugar, 1 egg, and 1 teaspoon vanilla; beat well. Sift together 1 cup sifted all-purpose flour, ½ teaspoon baking powder, and ¼ teaspoon *each* salt and soda; stir into cereal mixture. Add ¾ cup flaked coconut; spread batter in greased 8x8x2-inch baking pan. Bake at 350° for 20 to 25 minutes. Cool; cut in 16 bars.

SCOTCH TEAS

- ½ cup butter or margarine
- 1 cup brown sugar
- 2 cups quick-cooking rolled oats
- ¼ teaspoon salt
- 1 teaspoon baking powder

Combine butter and sugar in saucepan; cook and stir till butter melts. Stir in remaining ingredients; mix well. Pour into greased 8x8x2-inch baking pan. Bake in 350° oven 20 to 25 minutes. Cool; cut into bars. Makes 2 dozen.

COCONUT OATMEAL COOKIES

  2 cups sifted all-purpose flour
  1 cup granulated sugar
  1 teaspoon baking powder
  1 teaspoon soda
  ½ teaspoon salt
    . . .
  1 cup brown sugar
  1 cup shortening
  2 eggs
  ½ teaspoon vanilla
  1½ cups quick-cooking rolled oats
  1 cup chopped California walnuts
  1 cup flaked coconut

Sift together flour, granulated sugar, baking powder, soda, and salt. Add brown sugar, shortening, eggs, and vanilla; beat well. Stir in oats, walnuts, and coconut.

Roll dough in small balls. Dip tops in granulated sugar. Place on ungreased cookie sheet. Bake in a moderate oven (375°) for 12 to 14 minutes. Makes about 5½ dozen cookies.

CRUNCH COOKIES

Honey-flavored and crunchy with cereal—

  ½ cup shortening
  ½ cup granulated sugar
  ½ cup honey
  1 egg
  2 tablespoons milk
    . . .
  1½ cups sifted all-purpose flour
  1 teaspoon salt
  1 teaspoon cinnamon
  ½ teaspoon soda
  1 cup shredded wheat cereal,
    crumbled
  ½ cup chopped California walnuts
  1 cup raisins

Cream together shortening, sugar, honey, egg, and milk. Sift together flour, salt, cinnamon, and soda; add to creamed mixture. Stir in shredded wheat cereal, nuts, and raisins. Drop from teaspoon onto greased cookie sheet. Bake in a moderate oven (375°) for 12 to 13 minutes, or till lightly browned. Cool slightly before removing from cookie sheet. Then cool on rack. Makes about 5 dozen cookies.

BRAN APRICOT SQUARES

  ½ cup dried apricots
  1 cup water
  ½ cup butter or margarine
  ¼ cup granulated sugar
  ½ cup sifted all-purpose flour
  ¾ cup whole bran cereal
  2 eggs
  1 cup brown sugar
  ½ teaspoon vanilla
  ½ cup sifted all-purpose flour
  ½ teaspoon baking powder
  ½ teaspoon salt
  ½ cup chopped California walnuts

Dice apricots and add water. Simmer covered 10 minutes; drain. Set aside to cool. Cream butter and ¼ cup sugar. Stir in ½ *cup* flour and bran. Press over bottom of 9x9x2-inch baking pan. Bake at 350° for 15 minutes.

Meanwhile, beat eggs till thick and lemon-colored. Stir in brown sugar and vanilla. Sift together dry ingredients; add to egg mixture. Stir in cooked apricots and walnuts. Pour over baked bran layer. Bake in a moderate oven (350°) for 25 to 30 minutes. Cool; cut in squares or bars. Makes about 1½ dozen squares.

CEREALSNAPS

  ½ cup butter or margarine
  ½ cup brown sugar
  ½ cup granulated sugar
  1 egg
  1 teaspoon vanilla
  1¼ cups sifted all-purpose flour
  ½ teaspoon baking powder
  ½ teaspoon soda
  ½ teaspoon salt
  2 cups crisp rice cereal
  1 3½-ounce can (1⅓ cups) flaked
    coconut

Cream butter with sugars; add egg and vanilla, creaming till light and fluffy. Sift together flour, baking powder, soda, and salt; stir into creamed mixture. Stir in cereal and coconut. Shape in ¾-inch balls; place about 2½ inches apart on ungreased cookie sheet. Bake at 350° about 10 minutes or till lightly browned. Cool slightly; remove from pan. Cool on rack. Makes about 5 dozen cookies.

OATMEAL COOKIES

1 cup shortening
1½ cups brown sugar
2 eggs
½ cup buttermilk or sour milk*
1¾ cups sifted all-purpose flour
1 teaspoon soda*
1 teaspoon baking powder*
1 teaspoon salt
1 teaspoon cinnamon
1 teaspoon nutmeg
3 cups quick-cooking rolled oats
1 cup raisins
½ cup chopped California walnuts

Cream shortening, sugar, and eggs together till light and fluffy. Stir in buttermilk. Sift together dry ingredients; stir into creamed mixture. Stir in oats, raisins, and nuts. Drop from tablespoon 2 inches apart on lightly greased cookie sheet. Bake in hot oven (400°) about 8 minutes. Cool slightly; remove from pan. Makes about 5 dozen cookies.

*Or use sweet milk; reduce soda to ¼ teaspoon; use 2 teaspoons baking powder.

Oatmeal Cookies dotted with raisins just as you remember them from childhood days. Pebble-topped chewy cookies with lots of spice. Why not treat your family to these classics?

CHOCOLATE OAT COOKIES

Sift together 1 cup sifted all-purpose flour, ½ teaspoon soda, ½ teaspoon salt, and 1 cup granulated sugar into a bowl. Add ½ cup butter or margarine, softened, 1 egg, 1 teaspoon vanilla, and two 1-ounce squares unsweetened chocolate, melted and cooled. Blend mixture till smooth, about 2 minutes (dough will be very stiff). Add 1 cup quick-cooking rolled oats and ½ cup chopped pecans, mixing thoroughly till dough is well blended.

Shape by hand or drop from a teaspoon onto greased cookie sheet. Flatten with the bottom of a glass dipped in flour. Bake at 350° about 12 minutes. Makes 3 dozen cookies.

CRUNCHY DATE ROUNDS

½ cup butter or margarine
½ cup granulated sugar
¼ cup brown sugar
1 egg
1 teaspoon vanilla
1 cup sifted all-purpose flour
½ teaspoon baking powder
¼ teaspoon soda
½ teaspoon salt
½ cup chopped California walnuts
1 cup snipped pitted dates
1½ cups sugared cereal flakes,
   coarsely crushed (½ cup crushed)

Combine butter, sugars, egg, and vanilla; beat well. Sift together flour, baking powder, soda, and salt; gradually add to creamed mixture, blending well. Stir in nuts and dates. Drop from teaspoon into crushed cereal flakes, rolling to coat well. Bake about 2 inches apart on ungreased cookie sheet in moderate oven (375°) for 10 to 12 minutes, or till top springs back when lightly touched. Makes 3 dozen.

Nut-flavored favorites

CHINESE ALMOND COOKIES

2¾ cups sifted all-purpose flour
1 cup granulated sugar
½ teaspoon soda
½ teaspoon salt
1 cup butter, margarine, or lard
1 slightly beaten egg
1 teaspoon almond extract
⅓ cup blanched almonds, halved

Sift flour, sugar, soda, and salt together into bowl. Cut in butter till mixture resembles corn meal. Add egg and almond extract; mix well. Gather up with fingers; form into ball.

Roll to slightly less than ¼-inch thickness; cut with 2-inch round cutter. Place on ungreased cookie sheet about 2 inches apart. Place almond half atop each cookie. Bake in a slow oven (325°) for 15 to 20 minutes. Makes about 4 dozen cookies.

PEANUT-BUTTER CRINKLES

½ cup butter or margarine
½ cup chunk-style peanut butter
½ cup granulated sugar
½ cup brown sugar
1 egg
½ teaspoon vanilla
. . .
1¼ cups sifted all-purpose flour
¾ teaspoon soda
¼ teaspoon salt
. . .
Granulated sugar
Salted peanuts, halved

Thoroughly cream together butter, peanut butter, sugars, egg, and vanilla. Sift together flour, soda, and salt; blend into creamed mixture. Shape dough in 1-inch balls; roll in granulated sugar. Place 2 inches apart on greased cookie sheet. Press a few peanut halves on balls of dough. Bake cookies in moderate oven (375°) for 8 to 10 minutes. Cool slightly on cookie sheet; remove to rack to cool completely. Makes about 4 dozen cookies.

Crunchy Chinese Almond Cookies are natural go-alongs with fruit and green tea. For ease in making the cookies, form dough in 1-inch balls and flatten on cookie sheet with the bottom of a floured glass instead of rolling and cutting.

BRAZILIAN CREAMS

Cream ½ cup butter or margarine, and 1 cup brown sugar. Beat in 1 egg, and ½ teaspoon vanilla. Sift together 2 cups sifted all-purpose flour, ¾ teaspoon soda, ¾ teaspoon baking powder, ¼ teaspoon salt, ½ teaspoon cinnamon, and ¼ teaspoon nutmeg; add to creamed mixture alternately with ⅓ cup dairy sour cream. Stir in ½ cup chopped Brazil nuts. Drop from teaspoon 2 inches apart on greased cookie sheet. Bake in a hot oven (400°) for 8 to 10 minutes. Cool. Frost with Brown-butter Icing. Decorate with Brazil-nut Petals. Makes about 4 dozen cookies.

Brown-butter Icing: In a saucepan, heat and stir 3 tablespoons butter or margarine till browned; cool. Gradually add 2 cups sifted confectioners' sugar, 2 tablespoons milk, and 1 teaspoon vanilla; mix well.

Brazil-nut Petals: In a saucepan, cover *unshelled* Brazil nuts with cold water; boil 3 minutes, then drain. Cover with cold water; let stand 1 minute; drain. Crack and shell. Cover nuts with cold water and simmer 2 to 3 minutes; drain. With vegetable parer, cut paper-thin lengthwise slices.

CRISP PECAN SLICES

Bake-when-you-please refrigerator cookies—rich and lemon-y—

**¾ cup butter or margarine
1 cup granulated sugar
1 egg
1 teaspoon grated lemon peel
1 tablespoon lemon juice
2 cups sifted all-purpose flour
1 teaspoon baking powder
½ teaspoon salt
1 cup finely chopped pecans**

Thoroughly cream butter and sugar. Add egg, lemon peel, and juice; beat well. Sift together flour, baking powder, and salt; add to creamed mixture, mixing well. Stir in finely chopped nuts. Shape in rolls 2 inches in diameter. Chill thoroughly, about 2 hours.

Slice very thin and place on ungreased cookie sheet. Bake in a moderate oven (350°) for 10 to 12 minutes. Cool slightly before removing from pan. Makes about 5 dozen cookies.

PEANUT-BRAN BARS

No baking needed for these cookies—

**⅓ cup creamy peanut butter
1 cup granulated sugar
2 eggs, well beaten
½ cup peanuts
3 cups bran flakes**

. . .

**¼ cup semisweet chocolate pieces
1 tablespoon light corn syrup
2 teaspoons water**

Stir peanut butter, sugar, and eggs together in a skillet. Cook over medium heat until mixture comes to a boil and pulls away from sides of skillet, stirring constantly. Stir in peanuts and cereal, mixing thoroughly. Turn into a buttered 9x9x2-inch pan. Spread mixture evenly in pan. Chill until firm, 2 to 3 hours.

Combine semisweet chocolate pieces, corn syrup, and water in a small saucepan. Stir constantly over very low heat till chocolate is melted and mixture is smooth. Drizzle melted chocolate mixture over top of chilled mixture in a zigzag pattern. Cut bars. Makes 2 dozen.

CHOCOLATE NUT CLUSTERS

Like a nut cluster candy with a new twist—

Cream ¼ cup butter or margarine and ½ cup granulated sugar till light and fluffy. Add 1 egg and 1½ teaspoons vanilla; beat well. Blend in two 1-ounce squares chocolate, melted and cooled. Sift together ½ cup sifted all-purpose flour, ¼ teaspoon salt, and ¼ teaspoon baking powder; stir into creamed mixture. Stir in 2 cups broken California walnuts. Drop by small teaspoons on ungreased cookie sheet. Bake in a moderate oven (350°) for 10 minutes or till done. Makes about 3 dozen cookies.

BLACK WALNUT BALLS

**1 cup butter or margarine
1 cup sifted confectioners' sugar
¼ teaspoon salt
½ teaspoon vanilla
2 cups sifted all-purpose flour
1 tablespoon brandy
1 cup black walnuts, finely chopped**

Cream butter, sugar, salt, and vanilla together till fluffy. Stir in the flour. Add brandy and chopped nuts; mix well. Shape into ¾-inch balls using about ½ tablespoon dough per cookie; place on ungreased cookie sheet. Bake in a slow oven (325°) about 20 minutes, or until lightly browned. Makes about 6 dozen cookies.

BUTTER PECAN COOKIES

**1 cup butter or margarine
¾ cup brown sugar
¾ cup granulated sugar
2 eggs
1 teaspoon vanilla
2¼ cups sifted all-purpose flour
1 teaspoon soda
½ teaspoon salt
1 cup chopped pecans**

Cream butter and sugars till light. Beat in eggs and vanilla. Sift together dry ingredients; blend into creamed mixture. Stir in nuts. Drop from teaspoon on ungreased cookie sheet. Bake in a moderate oven (375°) about 10 minutes. Makes about 4 dozen cookies.

PARTY SPECTACULARS

COMPANY SPECIALS

TEA AND COFFEE TEMPTERS

CELEBRATION COOKIES

PARTY COOKIES FOR THE KIDS

TEEN WINNERS

HOSPITALITY IN A HURRY

HOLIDAY HIGHLIGHTS

WORLDWIDE CHRISTMAS FAVORITES

Great idea for a party—next time friends plan a trip, invite them over to say "bon voyage." Refreshments? Jam-topped Tasty Pastries, Creme-filled Cookies and Chocolate Mint Sails.

Company specials

TRI-LEVEL BROWNIES

½ cup sifted all-purpose flour
¼ teaspoon soda
¼ teaspoon salt
1 cup quick-cooking rolled oats
½ cup brown sugar
½ cup butter or margarine, melted

. . .

1 square (1 ounce) unsweetened
  chocolate, melted
¼ cup butter or margarine, melted
¾ cup granulated sugar
1 egg
⅔ cup sifted all-purpose flour
¼ teaspoon baking powder
¼ teaspoon salt
¼ cup milk
½ teaspoon vanilla
½ cup chopped California walnuts
1 recipe Frosting

For bottom layer: Sift together ½ cup flour, soda, and ¼ teaspoon salt; combine with oats and brown sugar. Stir in ½ cup melted butter. Pat mixture in bottom of 11x7x1½-inch baking pan; bake in a 350° oven for 10 minutes.

For middle layer: Combine chocolate, ¼ cup melted butter, and granulated sugar. Add egg; beat well. Sift together ⅔ cup flour, baking powder, and ¼ teaspoon salt; add alternately with milk and vanilla to chocolate mixture; fold in nuts. Spread batter over baked layer. Bake at 350° for 25 minutes longer.

For Frosting: Combine 1 square (1 ounce) unsweetened chocolate and 2 tablespoons butter in a small saucepan. Stir over low heat till chocolate melts. Remove from heat and add 1½ cups sifted confectioners' sugar and 1 teaspoon vanilla. Blend in enough hot water (about 2 tablespoons) to make almost pourable consistency. Spread over cooled brownies. Top with walnut halves. Makes 16 bars.

Special these are—Tri-level Brownies, Pecan Tassies, and Coconut Macaroons, which go so well with Irish Coffee or spicy Cappuccino.

PECAN TASSIES

Tiny tarts for festive entertaining—

1 3-ounce package cream cheese
½ cup butter or margarine
1 cup sifted all-purpose flour

. . .

1 egg
¾ cup brown sugar
1 tablespoon butter or margarine,
  softened
1 teaspoon vanilla
Dash salt

. . .

⅔ cup coarsely broken pecans

Cheese Pastry: Let cream cheese and ½ cup butter or margarine soften at room temperature; blend together. Stir in flour. Chill about 1 hour. Shape in 2 dozen 1-inch balls; place in ungreased 1¾-inch muffin pans. Press dough evenly against bottoms and sides of each.

Pecan Filling: Beat together egg, brown sugar, the 1 tablespoon butter, vanilla, and salt just till smooth. Divide *half* the pecans among pastry-lined pans; add egg mixture and top with remaining pecans. Bake in slow oven (325°) for 25 minutes or till filling is set. Cool before removing from pans. Makes 2 dozen.

COCONUT MACAROONS

Delicate, chewy party treats—

2 egg whites
Dash salt
½ teaspoon vanilla
⅔ cup granulated sugar
1 3½-ounce can (1⅓ cups) flaked
  coconut

Beat egg whites with dash salt and the vanilla till soft peaks form. Gradually add sugar; beating till stiff peaks form. Fold in flaked coconut. Drop batter by rounded teaspoon onto greased cookie sheet. Bake in a slow oven (325°) for about 20 minutes. Makes about 1½ dozen.

Tea and coffee tempters

STUFFED DATE DROPS

½ pound (about 39) pitted dates
About 39 pecan or walnut halves
¼ cup shortening
¾ cup brown sugar
1 egg
½ cup dairy sour cream
1¼ cups sifted all-purpose flour
½ teaspoon baking powder
½ teaspoon soda
¼ teaspoon salt

Stuff dates with nuts. Cream shortening and sugar till light; beat in egg. Stir in sour cream. Sift dry ingredients; add to creamed mixture. Stir in dates; drop onto greased cookie sheet (a date per cookie). Bake at 400° for 6 to 8 minutes; remove immediately; cool. Top with *Golden Frosting:* Lightly brown 6 tablespoons butter; remove from heat; cool. Gradually beat in 2 cups sifted confectioners' sugar and ¼ teaspoon vanilla. Slowly add hot water till of spreading consistency (about 2 tablespoons). If necessary, add hot water to thin. Makes about 3 dozen cookies.

LACE COOKIES

3 tablespoons granulated sugar
2 tablespoons light molasses
3 tablespoons butter or margarine
⅓ cup sifted all-purpose flour
½ teaspoon baking powder
½ teaspoon cinnamon
Dash salt
¼ cup finely chopped pecans

Combine sugar, molasses, butter, and 4 teaspoons water; heat to boiling. Remove from heat. Sift dry ingredients together. Blend into molasses mixture. Stir in nuts. Bake cookies two at a time on well greased cookie sheet, using 1 tablespoon batter for each. Bake at 325° about 8 minutes. Remove from oven and let cool *1 minute.* Loosen around edge with spatula, working toward center. Curve over greased custard cup. Makes about 12.

Serve miniature Spiced Sesame Bars for a snack or dessert with foreign flair. Their nutlike flavor will bring to mind the Turkish confection, Halvah. Why not brew a pot of Turkish coffee to carry out the idea?

SPICED SESAME BARS

½ cup sifted all-purpose flour
¼ teaspoon salt
¼ teaspoon soda
¼ teaspoon allspice
¼ teaspoon mace
½ teaspoon cinnamon
1 egg
¾ cup brown sugar
3 tablespoons butter or margarine, melted
¼ cup toasted sesame seed*

Sift together, flour, salt, soda, and spices; set aside. Beat egg; gradually add sugar and mix well. Stir in butter, then dry ingredients. Sprinkle half the sesame over bottom of greased 8x8x2-inch baking pan; pour in batter; top with remaining seeds. Bake at 350° for 20 minutes. Let cool; cut in bars. Makes 32.

*Spread seeds in shallow pan; heat at 350° for 10 minutes stirring occasionally.

Looking for something dainty? Apricot Fold-overs are just right for a bridge-party break or special tea party. The flavor combination is delightfully different—thin crisp cheese pastry around a sweet-tart apricot filling.

Frosty Date Balls are popular for any occasion that calls for a delicious cookie. They're a lot like festive shortbread, but filled with chopped dates and walnuts. Serve them with a lacy coating of confectioners' sugar.

APRICOT FOLD-OVERS

Delightfully different flavor combination of cheese and apricots—

½ cup butter or margarine
4 ounces sharp process American cheese, grated (1 cup)
1⅓ cups sifted all-purpose flour
2 tablespoons water

. . .

1 cup dried apricots
1 cup granulated sugar

Cream butter and cheese till light. Blend sifted flour into creamed mixture. Add water and mix well. Chill 4 to 5 hours. Meanwhile, cook dried apricots according to package directions. Drain well. Stir sugar into hot fruit; cook and stir till mixture boils and becomes smooth; cool. Divide chilled dough in half. Roll each half to 10-inch square; cut 2½-inch squares. Place 1 teaspoon apricot filling in each 2½-inch square; bring up diagonal corners and seal. Bake on ungreased cookie sheet at 375° for 8 to 10 minutes. Makes about 2½ dozen cookies.

FROSTY DATE BALLS

Cream ½ cup soft butter or margarine and ⅓ cup sifted confectioners' sugar. Stir in 1 tablespoon water and 1 teaspoon vanilla. Add 1¼ cups sifted all-purpose flour and dash salt. Mix well. Stir in ⅔ cup chopped pitted dates and ½ cup chopped California walnuts. Roll in 1-inch balls. Place 2½ inches apart on ungreased cookie sheet. Bake in a slow oven (300°) about 20 minutes, or till cookies are set but not brown. While warm, roll in confectioners' sugar. Makes about 2½ dozen cookies.

GREEK COOKIES

Cream 1 cup butter or margarine and ⅓ cup sifted confectioners' sugar; add 1 egg yolk and 1 tablespoon cognac; mix well. Gradually add 2 cups sifted all-purpose flour; chill 3 to 4 hours. Shape in 1-inch balls. Insert a whole clove in top of each. Bake on ungreased cookie sheet at 325° for 20 to 25 minutes. Cool; dust with sifted confectioners' sugar. Makes about 4 dozen cookies.

Celebration cookies

NUT-EDGED BUTTER SLICES

1½ cups sifted all-purpose flour
2 teaspoons baking powder
½ teaspoon salt
½ cup butter or margarine
⅔ cup granulated sugar
1 egg yolk
2 tablespoons light cream
1 teaspoon vanilla

. . .

½ cup toasted almonds, finely
   chopped
3 tablespoons granulated sugar
1 slightly beaten egg white

Sift together flour, baking powder, and salt. Cream butter and ⅔ cup sugar; add egg yolk, cream, and vanilla; beat well. Add flour mixture gradually, beating well. Shape dough on waxed paper into a 12x1½-inch roll. Chill 1 hour. Combine almonds and 3 tablespoons sugar. Brush chilled dough with egg white and roll in almond mixture, pressing nuts in firmly. Cut ¼-inch slices. Place on lightly greased cookie sheet; bake at 400° for 7 to 10 minutes. Makes about 4 dozen.

JAMWICH SUGAR COOKIES

Cream ⅔ cup shortening and ¾ cup granulated sugar; add 1 egg and 1 teaspoon vanilla; beat well. Sift together 2 cups sifted all-purpose flour, 1½ teaspoons baking powder, and ¼ teaspoon salt; stir into creamed mixture. Add 4 teaspoons milk. Divide dough in half; chill 1 hour. On surface lightly sprinkled with confectioners' sugar, roll to ⅛-inch thickness. Cut out cookies; cut centers from half the cookies. Bake on greased cookie sheet at 375° for 7 to 10 minutes. Cool. Spread whole cookies with tart red jelly. Frost remaining with pink Confectioners' Icing and press atop whole cookies. Makes 24.

Welcome guests with Nut-edged Butter Slices, Jamwich Sugar Cookies, and Russian Cookies.

RUSSIAN COOKIES

6 tablespoons butter or margarine
½ cup granulated sugar
1 egg yolk
1 tablespoon light cream
½ teaspoon vanilla
1 cup sifted all-purpose flour
1 teaspoon baking powder

. . .

½ cup apricot preserves
1 egg white
⅓ cup granulated sugar
1 teaspoon cinnamon
⅓ cup chopped nuts

Cream butter and ½ cup sugar. Add egg yolk, cream, and vanilla; beat well. Sift flour and baking powder together; add to creamed mixture Chill dough several hours. Divide dough in half; roll or pat each to 10x6x⅛-inch retangle on ungreased cookie sheet. Spread preserves over. Beat egg white till soft peaks form; gradually add sugar and cinnamon, beating to stiff peaks. Spread half the meringue over dough. Repeat with remaining dough and meringue; sprinkle nuts over both. Bake in a moderate oven (350°) for 12 minutes. Cool and cut into 1½x2-inch bars. Makes 2½ dozen cookies.

PEPPERMINT KISSES

2 egg whites
Dash salt
⅛ teaspoon cream of tartar
½ teaspoon peppermint extract
¾ cup granulated sugar
1 6-ounce package (1 cup) semisweet chocolate pieces

Beat egg whites, salt, cream of tartar, and peppermint extract till soft peaks form. Add sugar gradually, beating to stiff peaks. Fold in chocolate pieces. Cover cookie sheet with plain brown paper. Drop cookie mixture from teaspoon onto paper. Bake in a slow oven (325°) for 20 to 25 minutes. Remove from paper while slightly warm. Makes 2½ to 3 dozen cookies.

CONFECTION BARS

½ cup butter or margarine
¼ cup granulated sugar
⅓ cup cocoa (regular-type, dry)
1 teaspoon vanilla
1 slightly beaten egg
1 3½-ounce can flaked coconut
2 cups vanilla wafer crumbs
3 tablespoons milk
2 tablespoons *regular* vanilla
   pudding mix
½ cup butter or margarine
2 cups sifted confectioners'
   sugar
1 4-ounce bar sweet cooking
   chocolate
1 tablespoon butter or margarine

Combine ½ cup butter, ¼ cup sugar, cocoa, and vanilla in top of double boiler; cook and stir over hot water till blended. Add egg; cook 5 minutes. Stir in coconut and crumbs. Press into 9x9x2-inch pan; let stand 15 minutes.

Combine milk and dry pudding mix. Cream the ½ cup butter and confectioners' sugar. Add the pudding mixture and beat till smooth. Spread over first layer. Chill about 15 minutes or till firm. Melt sweet chocolate with the 1 tablespoon butter; cool and spread on second layer. Cut in squares. Makes 3 dozen.

TASTY PASTRIES

1 envelope active dry yeast
¼ cup *warm* water
1 10-ounce package pie crust mix
1 tablespoon granulated sugar
1 egg yolk
½ cup strawberry preserves, orange
   marmalade, *or* boysenberry jam

Soften yeast in warm water. Blend pie crust mix, sugar, egg yolk, and the softened yeast; mix well. Roll dough into balls the size of a small walnut. Place on ungreased cookie sheet. Make deep indentation in center of each ball, shaping into shells 1½ inches in diameter and ¼ inch deep. Spoon one teaspoon of jam into each shell. Let rise in warm place 1 hour.

Bake at 375° for 12 to 15 minutes. Cool slightly; remove from sheet. Makes 3 dozen.

REFRIGERATOR CRISPS

1 cup shortening
½ cup granulated sugar
½ cup brown sugar
1 egg
2 tablespoons milk
2¼ cups sifted all-purpose flour
½ teaspoon soda
½ teaspoon salt
1 teaspoon cinnamon
¼ teaspoon nutmeg
¼ teaspoon cloves
½ cup finely chopped California
   walnuts

Cream together shortening and sugars; add egg and milk; beat well. Sift together dry ingredients; stir into creamed mixture. Add nuts. Shape in rolls about 2½ inches in diameter. Wrap in waxed paper; chill thoroughly.

Slice about ¼ inch thick. Place 1 inch apart on lightly greased cookie sheet. Bake in moderate oven (375°) for 5 to 7 minutes or till delicately browned. Remove at once to cooling rack. Makes about 6 dozen cookies.

BRIGHT-EYED SUSANS

¾ cup butter or margarine
½ cup granulated sugar
1 egg
1 teaspoon vanilla
¼ teaspoon salt
1¾ cups sifted all-purpose flour
1 7-ounce package solid chocolate-
   mint candy wafers or chocolate
   nonpareils

Cream together butter, sugar, egg, vanilla, and salt. Stir in flour. Chill about 1 hour. Using about 2 teaspoons dough, shape in 1-inch balls. Place 2 inches apart on ungreased cookie sheet. Flatten each by pressing a wafer in center. Bake in hot oven (400°) for 8 to 10 minutes. Remove immediately from pan to cooling rack. Makes 3½ to 4 dozen.

Note: To substitute *solid pastel summer candy wafers:* flatten cookie dough balls with bottom of sugared glass. Bake in moderate oven (375°) for 3 minutes. Place *solid pastel summer candy wafer* in center of each. Bake about 4 minutes.

CREME-FILLED COOKIES

- 6 tablespoons chilled butter or margarine
- 1 cup sifted all-purpose flour
- 2½ tablespoons light cream
- ¾ cup sifted confectioners' sugar
- 1 tablespoon butter or margarine, softened
- ⅛ teaspoon almond extract
- 1 tablespoon light cream

With pastry blender or fork, cut the 6 tablespoons butter into flour till size of small peas. Sprinkle *1 tablespoon* cream over part of mixture. Gently toss with fork; push to one side of bowl. Sprinkle *next tablespoon* cream over dry part, mix lightly, push to moistened part at side. Repeat with remaining ½ tablespoon of cream till all is moistened. Gather dough up with fingers; form in ball.

For easier handling, divide dough in half. On lightly floured surface, roll to slightly less than ⅛ inch. Cut dough in 1½-inch squares with pastry wheel. Dip one side of each cookie in sugar. Place sugar side up, ½ inch apart, on ungreased cookie sheet. With fork, prick each cookie in parallel rows.

Bake in moderate oven (375°) about 8 minutes or till golden brown and puffy. Remove at once to cooling rack. When cookies are cool, sandwich with Almond Filling. Garnish with a dollop of Confectioners' Icing and a few pieces of sliced toasted almonds. Makes 2½ dozen.

Almond Filling: Thoroughly combine confectioners' sugar, the 1 tablespoon butter, almond extract, and the 1 tablespoon light cream (or enough for spreading consistency).

CHOCOLATE MINT SAILS

Prepare one recipe Fudge Brownies (see index listing) except omit the frosting or confectioners' sugar topping.

Combine 1 cup sifted confectioners' sugar, 2 tablespoons butter, softened, 1 tablespoon light cream, and ¼ to ½ teaspoon peppermint extract; beat well. Tint with green food coloring. Spread over cooled brownie layer; let stand till set. Melt one 1-ounce square unsweetened chocolate with 1 tablespoon butter. Drizzle over frosting. Chill till firm. Cut in bars or triangles. Makes 2 dozen.

COCONUT DIAMONDS

Buttery-rich flavor mingled with chewy coconut—

- 6 tablespoons butter or margarine, softened
- ¼ cup granulated sugar
- ¼ teaspoon salt
- 1 cup sifted all-purpose flour

• • •

- 2 eggs
- 1 teaspoon vanilla
- 1 cup brown sugar
- 2 tablespoons all-purpose flour
- ½ teaspoon salt
- 1 cup flaked coconut
- ½ cup coarsely chopped California walnuts

Cream together butter, ¼ cup sugar, and ¼ teaspoon salt. Stir in 1 cup flour. Pat onto bottom of 9x9x2-inch pan. Bake at 350° for 15 minutes or till lightly browned.

Meanwhile, beat eggs slightly; add vanilla. Gradually add 1 cup brown sugar, beating just till blended. Add 2 tablespoons flour and ½ teaspoon salt. Stir in coconut and walnuts. Spread over baked layer. Bake about 20 minutes longer or till toothpick comes out clean. Cool. Cut in diamonds. Makes about 1½ dozen.

DATE ORANGE BARS

- ¼ cup butter or margarine
- ½ cup brown sugar
- 1 egg
- 1 teaspoon grated orange peel

• • •

- 1 cup sifted all-purpose flour
- ½ teaspoon baking powder
- ½ teaspoon soda
- ¼ cup milk
- ¼ cup orange juice
- ½ cup chopped California walnuts
- ½ cup snipped pitted dates

Cream butter and sugar till fluffy. Add egg and peel; beat well. Sift together flour, baking powder, and soda; add to creamed mixture. Stir in milk, orange juice, nuts, and dates. Spread in greased 11x7x1½-inch pan. Bake in moderate oven (350°) for 25 minutes. Cool; sprinkle with confectioners' sugar.

Party cookies for the kids

What could be more fun than a grown-up tea party—especially when little ones can help with the treats! After Mother makes the cookie dough, tiny hands take over the decorating.

And what fun! Assorted candies, coconut, and raisins transform plain cookies into imaginary folk. At party time, wonderfully spicy Funnyface Cookies go great with milk.

FUNNY-FACE COOKIES

½ cup shortening
1 cup brown sugar
½ cup light molasses
½ cup milk
2 teaspoons vinegar
2½ cups sifted all-purpose flour
½ teaspoon soda
½ teaspoon salt
½ teaspoon ginger
½ teaspoon cinnamon
Wooden skewers
Raisins, assorted candies, coconut

Cream together shortening, brown sugar, and molasses. Stir in milk and vinegar. Sift together flour, soda, salt, ginger, and cinnamon; stir into molasses mixture. Drop by tablespoon about 2½ inches apart on lightly greased cookie sheet. Insert wooden skewer halfway into each mound of cookie dough. Stagger rows of cookies to leave room for the skewers. Use small spatula to spread dough around skewer if dough separates. Bake at 350° for 15 to 20 minutes or till done. Decorate faces with raisins, candies, and coconut. Secure with corn syrup. Let stand a few minutes before removing to cooling rack. Makes about 2 dozen.

LEMON-DROP COOKIES

½ cup butter or margarine
¾ cup granulated sugar
1 egg
1 tablespoon lemon juice
1½ cups sifted all-purpose flour
1 teaspoon baking powder
¼ teaspoon salt
¼ cup finely crushed lemon-drop
   candies

Thoroughly cream butter and sugar. Add egg and beat well. Add lemon juice. Sift together flour, baking powder, and salt. Gradually blend dry ingredients into creamed mixture; stir in crushed candy. Drop by teaspoon onto greased cookie sheet about 2 inches apart.

Bake in moderate oven (375°) about 10 to 12 minutes or until lightly browned. Cool slightly before removing from sheet. If desired, brush with corn syrup and garnish with additional crushed lemon-drop candies. Makes 3 dozen.

ORANGE GUMDROP CHEWS

Thoroughly mix 1½ cups gumdrop orange slices, cut up, one 3½-ounce can (1⅓ cups) flaked coconut, ½ cup chopped California walnuts, and 2 cups sifted all-purpose flour.

Beat 3 eggs with 1 tablespoon water till foamy. Gradually add 2 cups brown sugar and ½ teaspoon salt, beating till light and fluffy. Stir in gumdrop mixture. Spread evenly in greased 15½x10½x1-inch pan. Bake in moderate oven (375°) about 15 minutes or till done. Cool. Cut in bars. Makes 4 dozen.

MINT HIDEAWAYS

1 cup butter or margarine
1 cup granulated sugar
½ cup brown sugar
2 eggs
2 tablespoons water
1 teaspoon vanilla
3 cups sifted all-purpose flour
1 teaspoon soda
½ teaspoon salt
1 7-ounce package solid chocolate-
   mint candy wafers
California walnut halves

Cream butter and sugars. Beat in eggs, one at a time, then water and vanilla. Sift together dry ingredients; add to creamed mixture; mix thoroughly. Cover and refrigerate 2 hours.

Enclose a chocolate wafer in 1 tablespoon of chilled dough. Place on greased cookie sheet about 2 inches apart. Top each with walnut half. Bake in a moderate oven (375°) for 10 to 12 minutes. Makes 3 dozen cookies.

GOOBER COOKIES

Thoroughly cream ⅔ cup shortening, 1 cup brown sugar, and 1 egg. Sift together 1 cup sifted all-purpose flour, ½ teaspoon salt, ½ teaspoon baking powder, and ½ teaspoon soda; combine with creamed mixture. Stir in 1 cup quick-cooking rolled oats, ½ cup wheat flakes, and ½ cup chopped salted peanuts.

Roll into small balls; flatten slightly on greased cookie sheet. Bake in hot oven (400°) about 8 to 10 minutes or till done. Cool slightly; remove from sheet. Makes 3 dozen.

Let your small fry make a whole menagerie as pictured above—Emily Elephant, Gerry Giraffe, Roscoe Rabbit, Fillmore Fish, Katie Cat, and Bonnie Butterfly. Pieces on left show how cookie dough is cut and assembled for each.

BUTTERSCOTCH DROPS

½ cup butter or margarine
½ cup brown sugar
2 eggs
¼ cup milk
1 cup bran flakes
1¾ cups prepared biscuit mix
¼ teaspoon cinnamon
¼ teaspoon nutmeg
½ cup chopped California walnuts
½ cup raisins

Cream butter and sugar; beat in eggs and milk. Stir in remaining ingredients. Drop from teaspoon on ungreased cookie sheet. Bake at 375° for 10 minutes. Makes 4 dozen cookies.

A COOKIE ZOO

All it takes is a roll of commercial refrigerated cookie dough to make animal cookie cutouts. Usually one or two very thin slices of dough are needed for each. After the rounds are cut, use a catsup lid and a paring knife to make the other pieces. Then put them together on a cookie sheet and press on silver decorettes or other tiny candies for eyes if desired, and follow package directions for baking time and temperature. Part of the fun is to invent new animal shapes by putting circles, strips, and wedges together in "helter-skelter" style.

Here are some hints that may help:
1. Cut off two thin slices at a time and return remaining cookie roll to refrigerator.
2. Don't press the parts together. Barely touching is close enough!
3. Cool cookies 3 minutes before moving.
4. If you make a little mistake, don't give up. It may turn out to be a new animal.

Now you're ready to start a cookie parade. It's easy to hold the cookies upright with slit marshmallows for stands. Or, make a cookie cage from an oatmeal box. Paste a piece of paper around the box and form the bars from colored tape. Best of all, draw a home for each animal with crayons or colored pencil.

COCOA-MINT WAFERS

1 tablespoon vinegar
¼ cup milk
• • •
½ cup shortening
1 cup granulated sugar
1 egg
¼ to ½ teaspoon peppermint extract
2 cups sifted all-purpose flour
½ cup cocoa (regular-type, dry)
½ teaspoon soda
¼ teaspoon salt

Add vinegar to milk. Thoroughly cream shortening and sugar. Add egg, extract, and milk. Sift together flour, cocoa, soda, and salt; add to creamed mixture, blending well. Shape in rolls about 2 inches in diameter. Wrap dough in waxed paper and chill 4 to 6 hours. Slice rolls into thin cookies and place on ungreased cookie sheet. Bake in a moderate oven (350°) for 6 to 8 minutes. Makes about 6 dozen cookies.

FLOWERPOT COOKIE CUPS

A momentous occasion like a child's birthday deserves a special dessert. Watch the grins when they see these specially designed treats!

6 cups puffed rice cereal
½ pound (32) large marshmallows
¼ cup butter or margarine
¼ teaspoon peppermint flavoring
Chocolate ice cream
Flowers made from gumdrops and
pipe cleaners

Place puffed rice cereal in shallow pan in moderate oven (350°) for 10 minutes. Turn into a large, greased bowl. Melt marshmallows and butter over very low heat, stirring till smooth; add peppermint flavoring.

Pour marshmallow mixture over cereal, mixing till all the cereal is coated. Press into bottom and sides of ten greased custard cups. (If mixture cools too fast, return to oven and heat slightly.) Cool; remove from cups; fill with chocolate ice cream (or a combination of your favorite flavors). Insert gumdrop flowers, if desired. Makes 10 cups.

Flowerpot Cookie Cups made from puffed rice cereal and filled with favorite flavors of ice cream are a special treat for a child's birthday party. Gumdrop flowers are good to eat too! Serve with mugs of hot chocolate or milk.

Children love this turtle. Gingersnaps or vanilla wafers form body. Frost underside and attach legs of elbow macaroni. A toothpick doubles as tail and anchor for head of puffed wheat.

Very special for the small fry is this jumbo cookie with a parade of animal cookies marching around edge. Insert tiny candles in snipped marshmallows and light just before serving.

Teen winners

DOUBLE PEANUT BUTTER COOKIES

1½ cups sifted all-purpose flour
½ cup granulated sugar
½ teaspoon soda
¼ teaspoon salt
½ cup shortening
½ cup creamy peanut butter
¼ cup light corn syrup
1 tablespoon milk

Sift together dry ingredients. Cut in shortening and peanut butter till mixture resembles coarse meal. Blend in syrup and milk. Shape into 2-inch roll; chill. Slice ⅛ to ¼ inch thick. Place half the slices on ungreased cookie sheet; spread each with ½ teaspoon peanut butter. Cover with remaining slices; seal edges with fork. Bake at 350° for about 12 minutes. Cool slightly; remove from sheet. Makes 2 dozen.

OATMEAL ROUNDS

1½ cups sifted all-purpose flour
½ teaspoon soda
¾ teaspoon salt
¾ cup brown sugar
1½ cups quick-cooking rolled oats
½ cup shortening
½ cup butter or margarine
1 teaspoon vanilla
Sliced almonds

Sift together flour, soda, and salt; stir in sugar and oats. Cut in shortening and butter till mixture is crumbly. Combine 2 tablespoons cold water and vanilla; sprinkle over mixture, tossing lightly with a fork till all is moistened. Shape dough in rolls 2 inches across. Wrap in waxed paper; chill. Slice *thinly*. Trim with almonds. Bake on greased cookie sheet at 350° for 8 to 10 minutes. Makes about 72.

Teen-agers reach again and again for Double Peanut Butter Cookies. They're great!

DOUBLE CHOCOLATE BARS

¼ cup butter or margarine
¾ cup granulated sugar
1 teaspoon vanilla
¼ cup light corn syrup
2 eggs
2 1-ounce squares unsweetened chocolate, melted and cooled
1 cup sifted all-purpose flour
½ teaspoon salt
½ teaspoon baking powder
½ 6-ounce package (½ cup) semi-sweet chocolate pieces
½ cup chopped California walnuts

Cream butter, sugar, and vanilla till fluffy; add syrup and continue creaming. Beat in eggs and chocolate. Sift together dry ingredients; stir into batter. Fold in chocolate pieces and walnuts. Spread in greased 9x9x2-inch baking pan; bake in a moderate oven (350°) about 25 minutes. Cut in bars when cool.

MAPLE SCOTCHIES

2 cups sifted all-purpose flour
1½ cups brown sugar
½ cup butter or margarine, softened
1 teaspoon soda
½ teaspoon salt
1 slightly beaten egg
2 tablespoons milk
½ teaspoon maple flavoring
½ cup chopped pecans
2 tablespoons instant cocoa (dry)

Combine flour and sugar. Cut in butter till mixture resembles fine crumbs. Reserve ¼ cup. Add soda and salt to remaining flour-sugar mixture; mix well. Blend in egg, milk, and maple flavoring. Mix with pastry blender to form dough. Stir in pecans. Combine ¼ cup flour-sugar mixture with cocoa. Shape dough into balls, using rounded teaspoon of dough for each. Roll in cocoa mixture. Place 3 inches apart on cookie sheet. Bake at 375° for 10 to 12 minutes. Makes 4 dozen.

Hospitality in a hurry

Easy? You're right! These recipes are short-cuts to entertaining or everyday eating. On the top tier are sugar-coated Browned Butter Nuggets and Quick Sandwich Cookies made from refrigerated cookies. On the lower tier are Candlestick Bars and Chocolate Yummies with ready-to-spread frosting swirled atop, and Coconut Cake Bars with Marzipan toppers.

QUICK SANDWICH COOKIES

Cut 1 roll refrigerated slice-and-bake sugar cookies into 13 slices of about ¾-inch thickness. Cut each slice into quarters. Place 2 inches apart on ungreased cookie sheet and bake at 375° for about 9 minutes. Remove from oven. Top each of half the slices with a pecan half (about ½ cup). Top each of the remaining cookies with about 10 semisweet chocolate pieces (about ½ cup). Return to 375° oven for about 1 minute. Remove from oven; spread softened chocolate evenly over the chocolate-topped cookies. Top each with a pecan-topped cookie. Makes 26 sandwich cookies.

CANDLESTICK BARS

1 14-ounce package gingerbread mix
1 8-ounce can (1 cup) applesauce
½ cup raisins
1 4-ounce jar (½ cup) chopped mixed candied fruits and peels
1 14-ounce package white creamy-type frosting mix
2 tablespoons lemon juice

Combine gingerbread mix and applesauce. Beat 2 minutes at medium speed with electric mixer or 2 minutes with spoon. Stir in raisins and fruits and peels. Spread in greased 15½x 10½x1-inch pan. Bake at 375° for 15 minutes. Prepare frosting according to package directions, substituting the lemon juice for half the liquid. Spread on cooled cookies. Cut in 1x1½-inch bars. Decorate with gumdrop "candlesticks." Makes about 8 dozen.

BROWNED BUTTER NUGGETS

Toast one 2⅞-ounce package (about 2½ dozen) whole shelled filberts in 325° oven for 10 minutes. Brown ½ cup butter or margarine in saucepan. Add ¼ cup sifted confectioners' sugar and ½ teaspoon vanilla. Cool. Blend in 1¼ cups sifted all-purpose flour. Shape a rounded teaspoon of dough around each filbert to form balls. Place on ungreased cookie sheet. Bake at 325° for 20 minutes. Cool slightly on cookie sheet; remove. When cool, sift additional confectioners' sugar over cookies. Makes about 2½ dozen nuggets.

CHOCOLATE YUMMIES

1 4-ounce package chocolate pudding mix (regular type)
2 cups packaged biscuit mix
½ cup granulated sugar
1 slightly beaten egg
¼ cup milk
¼ cup butter or margarine, melted
1 teaspoon vanilla
1 3½-ounce can (1⅓ cups) flaked coconut
Refrigerated ready-to-spread creamy chocolate frosting
California walnut halves

Combine pudding mix (dry), biscuit mix, and sugar. Beat in next four ingredients. Stir in coconut. Drop from teaspoon onto ungreased cookie sheet. Bake at 350° for 11 to 13 minutes. Remove to cooling rack. Spread cooled cookies with frosting; top with nut halves. Makes about 3 dozen cookies.

COCONUT CAKE BARS

Prepare 1 package 1-layer-size yellow cake mix according to package directions. Pour batter into greased 9x9x2-inch pan. Bake at 350° for about 25 minutes, or till done. Cool.

While cake is cooling, gradually add ½ cup honey to ½ cup softened butter or margarine, beating till fluffy. Remove cake from pan; trim outside edges. Cut into 2x1-inch bars. Spread sides and top of each bar with honey-butter mixture. Roll in one 7-ounce package flaked coconut, toasted. Top each with a Marzipan strawberry. Makes 2½ dozen.

CARAMEL CHEWS

Place 36 (10 ounces) vanilla caramels and 3 tablespoons light cream in top of a double boiler over simmering water; heat till caramels melt; stir occasionally. Toss together 1 cup corn flakes, 2 cups crisp rice cereal, 1 cup flaked coconut, ½ cup chopped California walnuts, and ½ cup raisins. Pour caramel mixture over. Mix thoroughly. With buttered fingers, press rounded tablespoons of mixture lightly into balls. Place on waxed paper. Makes about 4 dozen confection cookies.

UNBAKED CARAMEL COOKIES

In a large saucepan, combine 2 cups granulated sugar, ¾ cup butter or margarine, and one 6-ounce can (⅔ cup) evaporated milk. Bring mixture to a rolling boil, stirring frequently. Remove from heat and add one 3⅝- or 4-ounce package *instant* butterscotch pudding mix and 3½ cups quick-cooking rolled oats; mix together thoroughly. Cool 15 minutes; drop dough from teaspoon onto waxed paper-lined tray. Makes about 5 dozen cookies.

COCONUT-BIT SQUARES

    1 package 1-layer-size white
        cake mix
    1 3½-ounce can (1⅓ cups)
        flaked coconut
    ¼ cup granulated sugar
    1 egg
    1 tablespoon milk
    ¼ teaspoon vanilla
    ½ cup semisweet chocolate pieces

Combine cake mix, coconut, sugar, egg, milk, and vanilla in mixing bowl. Blend together on low speed of electric mixer. Pat into greased and floured 9x9x2-inch baking pan. Sprinkle chocolate pieces over top. Bake in a moderate oven (350°) about 25 minutes. Cut into squares or bars while warm. Serve when cool.

CAKE MIX PRONTO COOKIES

    1 package 2-layer-size yellow
        cake mix
    ¼ cup soft butter or margarine
    ⅓ cup milk
    1 egg
    ½ teaspoon maple flavoring
            • • •
    1 6-ounce package (about 1 cup)
        semisweet chocolate pieces
    ½ cup chopped California walnuts

Combine cake mix, butter, milk, egg, and flavoring; beat until smooth. Stir in chocolate and nuts. Drop from teaspoon onto greased cookie sheet. Bake at 375° about 12 minutes. Let stand a few seconds before removing from sheet. Makes about 4½ dozen cookies.

Three cheers from the sweet-tooth crowd for confection-like Unbaked Caramel Cookies. These treats are made from an instant butterscotch pudding mix right in the saucepan.

GLORIFIED GRAHAMS

    24 graham-cracker squares
    ½ cup butter or margarine, melted
    ½ cup brown sugar
    1 cup chopped pecans

Line a 15½x10½x1-inch jellyroll pan with 24 graham-cracker squares. Mix butter and brown sugar; spoon over graham crackers. Sprinkle with nuts. Bake at 350° about 12 minutes. Break into squares. Makes 2 dozen cookies.

CHOCOLATE HAYSTACKS

    2 cups granulated sugar
    ⅓ cup cocoa (regular-type, dry)
    ½ cup milk
    ½ cup butter or margarine
    3½ cups quick-cooking rolled oats
    1 cup flaked coconut
    ½ cup chopped California walnuts
    ½ teaspoon vanilla
    Dash salt

In saucepan bring first 4 ingredients to a full boil. Remove from heat; stir in remaining ingredients. Drop quickly from teaspoon on waxed paper; cool. Makes about 48.

LAYER BAR COOKIES

½ cup butter or margarine
1 cup graham-cracker crumbs
1 6-ounce package (1 cup) semisweet chocolate pieces
1 6-ounce package (1 cup) butterscotch pieces
1 3½-ounce can (1⅓ cups) flaked coconut
½ cup chopped California walnuts
1 15-ounce can (1⅓ cups) sweetened condensed milk

Melt butter in a 13x9x2-inch pan. Sprinkle crumbs evenly over butter. Layer top with chocolate pieces, butterscotch pieces, coconut, and nuts. Pour condensed milk over all. Bake at 350° for 30 minutes; cool; cut in bars.

PEANUT BRITTLE COOKIES

1 stick pie crust mix
¾ cup brown sugar
½ teaspoon vanilla
1 slightly beaten egg
½ cup chopped peanuts

Prepare pie crust mix according to package directions. Blend in brown sugar and vanilla. Add egg and ¼ *cup* chopped peanuts.

Spread mixture on a well-greased and floured 17x14-inch cookie sheet to 10x13-inch rectangle. Top with remaining chopped peanuts.

Bake in moderate oven (350°) for 15 to 17 minutes. *Loosen edges as soon as cookie sheet is removed from oven;* cool on sheet. Cut.

EASY MACAROONS

Goes together in a wink—only 3 ingredients!—

2 8-ounce packages shredded coconut
1 15-ounce can (1⅓ cups) sweetened condensed milk
2 teaspoons vanilla

Mix ingredients. Drop from teaspoon onto *well-greased* cookie sheet. Bake in moderate oven (350°) for 10 to 12 minutes. Cool slightly; remove to rack. Makes about 4 dozen cookies.

RAISIN OATMEAL COOKIES

1 package 2-layer-size yellow cake mix
2 cups quick-cooking rolled oats
½ teaspoon salt
1 teaspoon cinnamon
½ teaspoon nutmeg
1 1-pound 6-ounce can raisin pie filling
2 eggs
¼ cup salad oil
1 cup chopped California walnuts

Combine all ingredients except nuts in a large bowl. Beat till blended. Stir in the nuts. Drop from a spoon onto a greased cookie sheet, using about 2 tablespoons dough for each. Bake in a moderate oven (350°) 15 to 17 minutes. Makes 5 dozen large cookies.

CREME DE MENTHE BALLS

2½ cups finely crushed vanilla wafers (about 60)
1 cup sifted confectioners' sugar
2 tablespoons cocoa (regular-type, dry)
1 cup finely chopped California walnuts
¼ cup light corn syrup
¼ cup white creme de menthe
Granulated sugar

Combine first 4 ingredients. Stir in corn syrup and creme de menthe. Add a few drops of water if necessary to form mixture in 1-inch balls. Roll in granulated sugar. Store in tightly covered container. Makes 3½ dozen.

CRANBERRY CHEWS

Beat 2 eggs, ¾ cup sugar, 1 tablespoon lemon juice, and ¼ teaspoon nutmeg till light and fluffy. Stir in 1½ cups prepared biscuit mix. Cut one 8-ounce can jellied cranberry sauce into ¼-inch cubes; fold into batter with 1 cup chopped pecans. Spread in well-greased and floured 13x9x2-inch baking pan. Bake at 350° for 20 to 25 minutes. Sift confectioners' sugar over top. Cut in thin bars while slightly warm. Makes about 3 dozen cookies.

Holiday highlights

JAM THUMBPRINTS

Cream together ⅔ cup butter or margarine and ⅓ cup granulated sugar until fluffy. Add 2 egg yolks, 1 teaspoon vanilla, and ½ teaspoon salt; beat well. Gradually add 1½ cups sifted all-purpose flour, mixing well.

Shape dough in ¾-inch balls; dip in 2 slightly beaten egg whites, then roll in ¾ cup finely chopped California walnuts. Place 1 inch apart on greased cookie sheet. Press down center of each with thumb.

Bake cookies in moderate oven (350°) for 15 to 17 minutes or till done. Cool slightly; remove from sheet and cool on rack. Just before serving use ⅓ cup cherry or strawberry preserves, or currant jelly to fill centers of cookies. Makes about 3 dozen cookies.

SWEDISH GINGER COOKIES

Cream 1 cup butter and 1½ cups granulated sugar. Add 1 egg; beat till fluffy. Add 1½ tablespoons grated orange peel, 2 tablespoons dark corn syrup, and 1 tablespoon water; mix. Sift together 3¼ cups sifted all-purpose flour, 2 teaspoons soda, 2 teaspoons cinnamon, 1 teaspoon ginger, and ½ teaspoon cloves. Stir into creamed mixture; chill.

On lightly floured surface, roll to ⅛-inch thickness. Sprinkle dough with granulated sugar; press in lightly with rolling pin. Cut with floured scalloped, or diamond, cutter. Place 1 inch apart on ungreased cookie sheet. Top each with toasted blanched almond. Bake at 375° for 8 to 10 minutes. Cool slightly before removing from pan. Makes about 8 dozen cookies.

Jam Thumbprints and Swedish Ginger Cookies —delicious nibbles when friends drop by for a jolly cup or when the family is gathered round a glowing fire. For gaily decorated Swedish Ginger Cookies, trim with mint patties and Christmas star candies secured with frosting.

Gingerbread Boys on the run double as decorations and snacks for the children. Bamboo skewers are baked right in the cookies. **Easy Sugarplums** on plate: Dip marshmallows in warm milk and then roll in colored sugar.

SNOWY CINNAMON STARS

Mix ⅔ cup granulated sugar, 1 teaspoon cinnamon, and ½ teaspoon grated lemon peel. Beat 2 egg whites till soft peaks form. Gradually add cinnamon-sugar mixture; continue beating until very stiff peaks form (about 10 minutes). Fold in 1¾ cups ground almonds. Chill dough several hours.

On lightly floured surface, roll dough to ⅛-inch thickness. Cut with 2½-inch star cutter. Place on well-greased cookie sheet. Frost with Meringue, spreading it to the points. Trim with silver candies. Bake in slow oven (325°) for 12 to 15 minutes. Remove from cookie sheet at once and cool on rack.

Meringue: Beat 1 egg white till soft peaks form. Gradually add 1 cup sifted confectioners' sugar, beating after each addition. Continue beating mixture until stiff peaks form. Frost cookies. Makes about 3 dozen cookies.

GINGERBREAD BOYS

1 cup shortening
1 cup granulated sugar
1 egg
1 cup molasses
2 tablespoons vinegar
5 cups sifted all-purpose flour
1½ teaspoons soda
½ teaspoon salt
2 to 3 teaspoons ginger
1 teaspoon cinnamon
1 teaspoon cloves

Thoroughly cream shortening with sugar. Stir in egg, molasses, and vinegar; beat well. Sift together dry ingredients; stir into molasses mixture. Chill at least 3 hours.

On lightly floured surface, roll dough to ⅛-inch thickness. Cut with a gingerbread-boy cutter (or draw your own pattern). Place 1 inch apart on greased cookie sheet.* Use red cinnamon candies for faces and buttons. Bake in moderate oven (375°) for 5 to 6 minutes. Cool slightly; remove from cookie sheet and cool on rack. Makes 5 dozen 4-inch cookies.

When thoroughly cool, trim with *Confectioners' Icing:* To 2 cups sifted confectioners' sugar, add only enough light cream to make mixture that will go through pastry tube easily but still hold its shape.

*For cookies that will stand up, bake gingerbread boys with "built-in" skewers: Arrange bamboo skewers on cookie sheet; place gingerbread boy on each so skewer is ⅓ the way up back of cookie. Bake cookies as above. To serve, stick skewers into apples.

MAILING TIPS

Choose fairly moist, non-fragile cookies such as fruit-filled drop or bar cookies, brownies, etc. Avoid frostings that become sticky at room temperature. Wrap each cookie individually, or wrap in pairs back to back, in clear plastic wrap.

Pack tightly into metal cans or boxes. Bake bar cookies in foil-ware pans; mail in the baking pan. Pack metal containers in a strong cardboard box cushioned with crushed newspaper, confetti, or popcorn. Tie securely and label the package clearly.

COCONUT DAINTIES

1 cup butter or margarine
¼ cup sifted confectioners' sugar
2 teaspoons vanilla
1 tablespoon water
2 cups sifted all-purpose flour
1 cup chopped pecans
1 recipe Confectioners' Icing
Tinted coconut

Thoroughly cream butter, sugar, and vanilla. Stir in water. Add flour and mix well. Stir in nuts. Shape in 1-inch balls. Bake 1 inch apart on ungreased cookie sheet at 300° about 20 minutes, or till firm to touch. Cool thoroughly before removing from pan.

Confectioners' Icing: Combine 2 cups sifted confectioners' sugar, dash salt, and 1 teaspoon vanilla; add enough light cream to make spreading consistency. Dip cookies in icing, then in tinted coconut: Shake 1⅓ cups flaked coconut in covered jar with few drops food coloring. Makes 4 dozen cookies.

Sandies: Omit icing and tinted coconut; roll cookies in confectioners' sugar.

FRUITCAKE COOKIES

¼ cup butter or margarine
¾ cup brown sugar
1 egg
¼ cup evaporated milk
1 teaspoon lemon juice
1 cup sifted all-purpose flour
¼ teaspoon *each* soda and salt
½ teaspoon cinnamon
½ teaspoon cloves
½ teaspoon allspice
Dash nutmeg
1 cup chopped mixed candied fruits
   and peels
¾ cup raisins
1 cup chopped pecans

Cream butter and sugar till fluffy; beat in egg. Combine milk and lemon juice; gradually add to creamed mixture. Reserve ¼ cup flour. Sift remaining flour with soda, salt, and spices; stir into creamed mixture. Mix reserved flour with fruits and pecans; blend into dough. Drop by teaspoon on lightly greased cookie sheet. Bake at 375° for 10 to 12 minutes. Makes 60.

HOLIDAY FUN WITH SUGAR COOKIES

Decorating sugar cookies provides entertainment for the whole family. Here are just a few ideas to use as starters—then use your imagination to add new twists.

Before baking, sprinkle cookies with colored sugar, candy decorettes, crushed hard peppermint stick candy, or gumdrops (sliced or whole). To make poinsettia cookies, cut red candied cherries in eighths; arrange 3 pieces on each cookie to look like petals.

For cameo cutouts, divide dough and tint different colors. Roll and cut out designs. Then with tiny cutter or thimble make cutouts in center of each cookie. Switch cutouts to make contrasting centers.

To decorate cookies with fancy frosting, add enough light cream to sifted confectioners' sugar to make spreading consistency. Tint icing various colors with food coloring. Frost cookies after they have cooled. Pipe on different colored designs with cake decorator or decorate with an assortment of gay candies.

SUGAR COOKIES

⅔ cup shortening
¾ cup granulated sugar
1 teaspoon vanilla
   • • •
1 egg
4 teaspoons milk
   • • •
2 cups sifted all-purpose flour
1½ teaspoons baking powder
¼ teaspoon salt

Thoroughly cream shortening, sugar, and vanilla. Add egg; beat till light and fluffy. Stir in milk. Sift together flour, baking powder, and salt; blend into creamed mixture. Divide dough in half. Chill 1 hour.

On lightly floured surface, roll to ⅛-inch thickness.* Cut in desired shapes with cutters. Decorate as desired. Bake on greased cookie sheet in moderate oven (375°) about 6 to 8 minutes. Cool slightly; remove from pan. Cool on rack. Makes about 2 dozen cookies.

*Roll only half of dough at a time; keep remainder chilled for easier rolling.

Worldwide Christmas favorites

SPRINGERLE

> 4 eggs
> 1 pound (about 4 cups) sifted
>   confectioners' sugar
> 20 drops anise oil
> 4 cups sifted all-purpose flour
> 1 teaspoon soda
> Crushed anise seed

With electric mixer, beat eggs till light. Gradually add sugar; continue beating on high speed 15 minutes or till mixture is like soft meringue. Add anise oil. Sift together flour and soda; blend into mixture on low speed. Cover bowl tightly with aluminum foil and let stand for 15 minutes (for easier handling).

Divide dough in thirds. On lightly floured surface, roll each piece in an 8-inch square, a little more than $1/4$ inch thick. Let stand 1 minute. Dust springerle rolling pin or mold lightly with flour; roll or press hard enough to make a clear design. With sharp knife, cut the cookies apart. Place on lightly floured surface; cover with a towel and let stand overnight.

Grease cookie sheets and sprinkle each with $1\frac{1}{2}$ to 2 teaspoons crushed anise seed. Brush excess flour from cookies; with finger, rub underside of each cookie very lightly with cold water and place on cookie sheets. Bake at 300° about 20 minutes or till light straw color. Makes about 6 dozen cookies.

For best eating, store cookies in an airtight container for a couple of days.

Prize gift cookies add a delightful personal touch to holiday greetings. Springerle, imprinted from hand-carved molds, are delicately flavored with anise. Austrian Linzer Cookies feature raspberry jam peeking through a rich, almond crisscross lattice. The many festive shapes of Spritz cookies are gayly decorated with colored sugar. What tasty Christmas fare!

AUSTRIAN LINZER COOKIES

1½ cups sifted all-purpose flour
¼ cup granulated sugar
½ teaspoon baking powder
½ teaspoon salt
½ teaspoon cinnamon
½ cup brown sugar
½ cup butter or margarine
1 slightly beaten egg
⅓ cup blanched almonds, ground
½ cup red-raspberry jam
1 slightly beaten egg yolk
1 teaspoon water

Sift together flour, sugar, baking powder, salt, and cinnamon; stir in brown sugar. Cut in butter or margarine till mixture is crumbly. Add egg and ground almonds; mix with fork.

Reserve ½ cup mixture for lattice and into it mix 2 tablespoons additional all-purpose flour; chill 1 hour. Meanwhile press remaining mixture evenly into 9x9x2-inch baking pan. Spread with raspberry jam.

Roll out reserved chilled mixture on well-floured surface to ¼-inch thickness. Cut in strips a little less than ¼ inch wide. For lattice top, line up 11 strips across filling; then lay 11 strips diagonally across. Combine slightly beaten egg yolk and water; brush over lattice.

Bake in moderate oven (375°) about 25 minutes or till done. Cool. Cut in bars or squares.

SPRITZ

1½ cups butter or margarine
1 cup granulated sugar
1 egg
2 tablespoons milk
1 teaspoon vanilla
½ teaspoon almond extract
4 cups sifted all-purpose flour
1 teaspoon baking powder
Colored sugar

Thoroughly cream butter or margarine and sugar. Add egg, vanilla, and almond extract; beat well. Sift together flour and baking powder; add gradually to creamed mixture, mixing to a smooth dough. Do not chill.

Force dough through cookie press onto ungreased cookie sheet. Sprinkle with colored sugar, if desired. Bake in hot oven (400°) about 7 to 8 minutes. Cool. Makes about 5 dozen.

LEBKUCHEN

1 egg
¾ cup brown sugar
½ cup honey
½ cup dark molasses

• • •

3 cups sifted all-purpose flour
1¼ teaspoons nutmeg
1¼ teaspoons cinnamon
½ teaspoon soda
½ teaspoon cloves
½ teaspoon allspice
½ cup slivered almonds
½ cup chopped mixed candied
   fruits and peels, finely chopped
Lemon glaze

Beat egg; add brown sugar; beat till fluffy. Stir in honey and molasses. Sift together flour, nutmeg, cinnamon, soda, cloves, and allspice; add to first mixture; mix well. Stir in nuts, fruits and peels. Chill dough several hours. On floured surface, roll ¼ inch thick; cut in 3½x2-inch rectangles. Bake on greased cookie sheet in moderate oven (350°) about 12 minutes. Cool slightly; remove and cool on rack.

While cookies are still warm, brush with *Lemon Glaze:* Combine 1 slightly beaten egg white, 1 tablespoon lemon juice, ½ teaspoon grated lemon peel, dash salt, and 1½ cups sifted confectioners' sugar. Trim with Christmas stickers, if desired. Makes 2 dozen.

SCOTCH SHORTBREAD

1 cup butter, softened
½ cup granulated sugar
2½ cups sifted all-purpose flour

Cream together butter and sugar until light and fluffy. Stir in flour. Dough will be crumbly at first, but work in the flour by hand until dough becomes pliable. Chill several hours.

Divide dough in half. On ungreased cookie sheet, pat each half into a 7-inch circle. With fork prick each mound deeply to make 16 pie-shaped wedges. *Or* on floured surface, roll dough ¼ to ½ inch thick. Cut in 2x½-inch strips or with 1¾-inch cutter. Prick the center of each cookie with a fork.

Bake on ungreased cookie sheet at 300° about 30 minutes. Cool slightly; remove from pan. Makes 32 wedges or 42 cookies.

ROSETTES

2 eggs
1 tablespoon granulated sugar
¼ teaspoon salt
1 cup sifted all-purpose flour
1 cup milk
1 teaspoon vanilla

. . .

Confectioners' sugar

Combine eggs, sugar, and salt; beat well. Add flour, milk, and vanilla and beat smooth. Heat rosette iron in deep hot fat (375°) for 2 minutes. Remove; drain off excess fat.

Then dip hot iron into batter to ¼ inch from top of iron; dip at once into hot fat (375°). Fry rosette till golden, about ½ minute. Lift iron out; tip slightly to drain off any excess fat. With fork, push rosette off iron onto paper towels placed on rack. Reheat iron for 1 minute; make next rosette. Sift confectioners' sugar over cooled rosettes. Makes 3½ dozen.

SANDBAKELSER

1 cup butter or margarine
1 cup granulated sugar
1 egg
1 teaspoon almond extract
3 cups sifted all-purpose flour

. . .

1 cup apricot preserves
2 teaspoons lemon juice
¼ cup chopped candied red cherries
¼ cup toasted sliced almonds

Thoroughly cream butter or margarine and sugar. Add egg and almond extract; beat well. Stir in sifted flour. Pinch off small ball of dough and place in center of 2½-inch sandbakelse mold;* with your thumb, press dough evenly and as thinly as possible over bottom and sides. Place molds on cookie sheet.

Bake in moderate oven (350°) about 12 to 14 minutes or till lightly browned. Cool. To remove, invert molds and tap lightly. (Clean molds with dry cloth only.)

Just before serving, combine preserves, lemon juice, and cherries. Place teaspoon of mixture in each cookie tart. Stick in almonds or sprinkle over. Makes about 3½ dozen.

*They look like tiny fluted tart pans. If not available, use tiny foilware pans instead.

FATTIGMANN

6 egg yolks
¼ cup granulated sugar
1 tablespoon butter or margarine, melted
⅓ cup whipping cream, whipped
1 teaspoon ground cardamom
2 cups sifted all-purpose flour
½ teaspoon salt

Beat egg yolks till thick and lemon-colored; gradually beat in sugar. Gently stir in melted butter or margarine. Fold in whipped cream and cardamom. Sift together flour and salt; fold into egg yolk mixture, a little at a time, adding just enough to make a soft dough. Chill several hours or overnight.

Divide dough in half. On lightly floured surface, roll each half to ⅛-inch thickness. Cut rolled dough in long strips 1¼ inches wide, then slash diagonally at 4-inch lengths. Cut lengthwise slit in center of each and pull one end of cookie dough through.

Fry in deep hot fat (375°) about 1 to 1½ minutes or till very light golden brown; fry only a few at a time. Drain on paper towels. While warm, sprinkle with granulated sugar. Makes about 5 dozen cookies.

PFEFFERNUESSE

¾ cup light molasses
½ cup butter or margarine
2 beaten eggs

. . .

4¼ cups sifted all-purpose flour
½ cup granulated sugar
1¼ teaspoons soda
1½ teaspoons cinnamon
½ teaspoon cloves
½ teaspoon nutmeg
Dash pepper

In saucepan, combine molasses and butter. Cook and stir till butter melts. Cool to room temperature. Stir in eggs. Sift together flour, sugar, soda, cinnamon, cloves, nutmeg, and pepper. Add to molasses mixture; mix well. Chill several hours or overnight.

Shape chilled dough into 1-inch balls. Bake on greased cookie sheet in moderate oven (375°) for 12 minutes. Cool; roll in confectioners' sugar. Makes about 4½ dozen cookies.

SUMPTUOUS SWEETS

QUICK CANDIES

VELVETY SWEETS

SO-GOOD SOUTHERN PRALINES

FANTASTIC FUDGE

DIVINITY THAT'S DIVINE

HARD-CRACKIN' CANDIES

CRUNCHY CANDIED APPLES

POPCORN TRICKS

NUT AND FRUIT CONFECTIONS

There's nothing like homemade
candy for a gift with a personal touch.
Gay boxes offer Remarkable Fudge,
green and red Crystal-cut Candies, Spicy
Walnuts, and cherry-dotted Divinity.

Candy capers

Testing Candy. The best way to test the doneness of candy is to use a candy thermometer. Check the accuracy of the thermometer in boiling water each time it is used. If it registers above or below 212°, add or subtract degrees to make same allowance in recipe. Clip candy thermometer to pan after syrup boils (*bulb must be covered with boiling liquid, not just foam*).

If a candy thermometer is not available, follow the Cold Water Test. Remove pan from heat and immediately drop a few drops of boiling syrup from spoon into a cup of very cold (but *not* ice cold) water. Use fresh water and a clean spoon for each test. Form drops into a ball with fingers (its firmness indicates temperature of syrup—see chart below).

Candy Hints. When milk is an ingredient in the recipe, avoid scorching candy by cooking over medium heat. Candies made with water can be cooked over higher heat.

While candy is cooling (on wire rack) be sure that the candy is not jarred or the sugar will crystallize and the candy will be grainy.

If it's rainy outside or very humid, it's recommended that candies be cooked a degree or so above what is given in recipe.

To "repair" fudge that has become too stiff before it's poured into pan, knead with hands till it softens; then, press into buttered pan or shape in roll and slice. To "repair" fudge that doesn't set, stir in ¼ cup milk. Recook to given temperature; beat till right consistency.

TEMPERATURES AND TESTS FOR CANDY

Temperatures (at Sea Level)	Stage	Cold Water Test
230° to 234°F	Thread	Syrup dropped from spoon spins 2-inch thread.
234° to 240°F	Soft ball	Syrup can be shaped into a ball but flattens when removed from water.
244° to 248°F	Firm ball	Syrup forms ball till pressed between fingers.
250° to 266°F	Hard ball	Syrup forms hard ball, although it is pliable.
270° to 290°F	Soft crack	Syrup separates into threads that are not brittle.
300° to 310°F	Hard crack	Syrup separates into hard, brittle threads.

Left: For this type thermometer, slide indicator to temperature given in recipe. Clip thermometer to pan so that *tip* is well covered by candy mixture and does not touch bottom of pan.
Right: Be sure that *bulb* of this type thermometer is well covered with candy mixture. For an accurate reading, bend down and read it at eye level.

Chocolate dipping

After centers are chocolate-dipped, draw fork across rim of pan to remove excess chocolate.

Caramels, nuts, candied fruits, or molded fondant may be chocolate-dipped. (Mold fondant centers the day before dipping so fondant won't leak through chocolate.) For best results, chocolate-dip on a dry, cool day and work in a room that is about 65° in temperature.

Use at least 1 pound grated candymaking chocolate (semisweet squares). Place over *hot, not boiling*, water (115° to 120°), with water touching top pan. Stir till melted.

Exchange hot water for cold in bottom of double boiler; stir and cool chocolate to 83°. Exchange cold water for warm (85°). Working rapidly, drop centers into chocolate, roll to coat centers, remove with fork; drop onto waxed paper over rack, bringing "string" of chocolate across top. (If chocolate becomes too stiff, heat as at first; continue dipping.)

Storing and freezing

Candy Storage. Fudge and fondant will keep fresh and creamy for several weeks if wrapped in waxed paper, aluminum foil, or clear plastic wrap. Then, store in an airtight container in a cool, dry place.

Keep chocolate-dipped candies in bonbon cups and store in a cool, dry place.

Taffies and caramels can be stored the same way as fudge. Wrap each piece individually to keep out moisture.

Divinity dries out quickly and is not a good keeper—so eat while fresh!

Freezing Candy. Homemade and commercially prepared candies freeze well. Wrap the candy box with aluminum foil or clear plastic wrap to protect candy. Before using, thaw unopened in the package to avoid moisture condensing on the candy and discoloring it.

Popcorn balls can also be frozen. Wrap each in clear plastic wrap. Toss wrapped balls in a polyethylene bag and store in the freezer until ready to use. Thaw in wrapper before serving.

A quick and easy way to freeze fudge is to turn it into a disposable aluminum foil pan just after it's beaten; wrap tightly and freeze.

Quick candies

PEANUT CEREAL CANDY

3 cups crisp rice cereal
1 cup salted peanuts
½ cup granulated sugar
½ cup light corn syrup
½ cup peanut butter
½ teaspoon vanilla

Mix cereal and peanuts; set aside. Combine sugar and syrup. Cook, stirring constantly, till mixture comes to a full rolling boil. Remove from heat. Stir in peanut butter and vanilla. Immediately pour syrup over cereal mixture, stirring gently to coat. Pat cereal evenly into buttered 8x8x2-inch pan. Cool; cut in 1x2-inch bars. Makes 32 bars.

DEWDROPS

1 3- or 3¼-ounce package *regular*
   vanilla pudding mix
1 cup granulated sugar
1 6-ounce can (⅔ cup) evaporated
   milk
   . . .
1 tablespoon butter or margarine
1 teaspoon vanilla
½ cup chopped California walnuts
¼ cup chopped candied cherries

Combine dry pudding mix, sugar, and milk in 2-quart saucepan. Cook and stir till mixture boils. Cook at full rolling boil for 5 minutes, stirring constantly. Remove from heat; add butter and vanilla. Beat at high speed in small bowl of electric mixer for 3 to 4 minutes or till mixture holds shape. Stir in nuts and cherries. Drop from teaspoon onto buttered cookie sheet. Top with cherry halves. Store in cool place. Makes 24.

Count on packaged foods to make all these candies in a jiffy. Pastel Mint Wafers begin with frosting mix; Peanut Cereal Candy, with peanut butter; cherry-topped Dewdrops, with pudding mix; and Caramel Snappers, with candy.

CARAMEL SNAPPERS

144 small pecan halves (about 1 cup)
36 light caramels
½ cup semisweet chocolate pieces,
   melted

Grease cookie sheet. On it arrange pecans, flat side down, in groups of 4. Place 1 caramel on each cluster of pecans. Heat in slow oven (325°) till caramels soften, about 4 to 8 minutes. (Watch carefully; various caramels melt at different rates.) Remove from oven; with buttered spatula, flatten caramel over pecans. Cool slightly; remove from pan to waxed paper. Swirl melted chocolate on top. Makes 36.

MINT WAFERS

3 tablespoons butter or margarine
3 tablespoons milk
1 14-ounce package white creamy-
   type frosting mix
Several drops oil of peppermint

Melt butter with milk in top of double boiler. Add frosting mix; stir till smooth. Cook over rapidly boiling water for 5 minutes, stirring occasionally. Add flavoring and desired food coloring. Drop from teaspoon onto waxed paper, swirling tops of candies with teaspoon. (Keep candy over hot water while dropping wafers. If mixture thickens, add few drops hot water.) Cool till firm. Makes 5 dozen.

QUICK PENUCHE

In heavy saucepan combine one 1-pint jar marshmallow creme, one 6-ounce can (⅔ cup) evaporated milk, ⅓ cup butter or margarine, 1¾ cups granulated sugar, and ¼ teaspoon salt. Stir over medium heat till mixture boils. Remove from heat. Add one 6-ounce package butterscotch pieces, stirring till smooth. Stir in 1 cup coarsely chopped California walnuts. Pour into buttered 8x8x2-inch pan. Chill till firm. Cut in squares. Makes 5 dozen.

SCOTCH CRUNCHIES

> 1 6-ounce package (1 cup)
>   butterscotch pieces
> 1 6-ounce package (1 cup)
>   semisweet chocolate pieces
> 1 3-ounce can (2 cups) chow mein
>   noodles
> 1 4½-ounce package (1 cup) salted
>   cashews

Melt butterscotch and chocolate pieces over hot water. Remove from heat. Stir in noodles and cashews. Drop by teaspoon onto waxed paper. Refrigerate until set. Makes about 4 dozen.

CHOCOLATE NUT PILLOWS

> 1 6-ounce package (1 cup) semisweet
>   chocolate pieces
> 1 tablespoon shortening
> ½ cup peanut butter
> 2 tablespoons confectioners' sugar
> 3 cups spoon-size shredded wheat
>   biscuits
> ½ cup finely chopped peanuts

Melt chocolate pieces and shortening over boiling water. Stir in peanut butter and sugar. Coat biscuits in chocolate; shake off excess. Roll in nuts. Cool on rack. Makes about 3 cups.

EASY CHOCOLATE FUDGE

> ½ cup butter or margarine
> 1 4-ounce package *regular*
>   chocolate pudding mix
> 1 3- or 3¼-ounce package *regular*
>   vanilla pudding mix
> ½ cup milk
> 1 1-pound box sifted confection-
>   ers' sugar (about 4 cups)
> ½ teaspoon vanilla
> ½ cup chopped California walnuts

In saucepan, melt butter; stir in dry pudding mixes and milk. Bring to boiling; boil for 1 minute, stirring constantly. Remove from heat; beat in sugar. Stir in vanilla and nuts. Pour into buttered 10x6x1½-inch baking dish. Garnish with walnut halves, if desired. Chill before cutting in 1½-inch squares. Makes 24.

PECAN ROLL

> 1 12-ounce package penuche fudge mix
> ½ pound caramels (about 28)
> ¼ cup milk
> 1½ cups chopped pecans

Prepare fudge mix according to package directions; cool. Roll into four rolls about 1 inch in diameter. Melt caramels with milk; spread rolls with caramel mixture; roll in pecans. Chill. Cut in ½-inch slices. Makes 32.

PEANUT CLUSTERS

> 1 4-ounce package *regular* chocolate
>   pudding mix
> 1 cup granulated sugar
> ½ cup evaporated milk
> 1 tablespoon butter or margarine
> 1 cup salted peanuts
> 1 teaspoon vanilla

Combine pudding mix, sugar, milk, and butter in heavy saucepan. Cook and stir over medium heat till mixture boils. Reduce heat; cook and stir 3 minutes. Remove from heat; quickly stir in nuts and vanilla. Beat till candy thickens and begins to lose its gloss. Drop from teaspoon into clusters on waxed paper. Makes 2 dozen.

Smooth, creamy, rich with milk chocolate flavor, Easy Chocolate Fudge combines convenience of mixes, tasty goodness of real fudge.

Velvety sweets

NOUGAT

1½ cups granulated sugar
1 tablespoon cornstarch
1 cup light corn syrup
½ cup water
. . .
2 egg whites
1 4-ounce jar red candied cherries,
    chopped (⅔ cup)

Grease 9x5x3-inch pan lightly, then dust with cornstarch. In large saucepan, combine sugar and 1 tablespoon cornstarch. Add corn syrup and water. Cook and stir till mixture dissolves. Continue cooking to soft-crack stage (286°), stirring as necessary to prevent sticking.

Meanwhile, beat egg whites with electric mixer until stiff peaks form. Slowly pour syrup into egg whites, beating constantly with mixer. Beat until mixture becomes stiff. Fold in cherries. Pack into loaf pan. Cut in 1-inch squares.

MARSHMALLOWS

2 envelopes (2 tablespoons) un-
    flavored gelatin
½ cup cold water
1 cup granulated sugar
1 cup light corn syrup
⅓ cup water
1 egg white

Soften gelatin in ½ cup cold water. In 2-quart saucepan, combine sugar, corn syrup, and ⅓ cup water. Cook to soft-ball stage (240°) stirring only until sugar dissolves. Remove from heat and stir in gelatin until dissolved. Set aside to cool for 10 minutes.

Beat egg white in small bowl of electric mixer to stiff peaks. Slowly add the syrup, beating on high speed till candy stands in soft peaks. Pour onto plain brown paper and spread into a 12x10-inch rectangle. Let stand overnight. Dust top with confectioners' sugar; turn over onto another piece of paper. Moisten brown paper and peel it off the candy. Makes about 1½ pounds of marshmallows.

CARAMELS

1 cup butter or margarine
1 pound (2¼ cups) brown sugar
Dash salt
1 cup light corn syrup
1 15-ounce can sweetened condensed
    milk
1 teaspoon vanilla

Melt butter in heavy 3-quart saucepan. Add brown sugar and salt; stir till thoroughly combined. Stir in light corn syrup; mix well. Gradually add milk, stirring constantly. Cook and stir over medium heat till candy reaches firm-ball stage (245°), about 12 to 15 minutes. Remove from heat; stir in vanilla. Pour into buttered 9x9x2-inch pan. Cool and cut into squares. Makes about 2½ pounds.

CHOCOLATE CARAMELS

Follow directions for Caramels given above except add two 1-ounce squares unsweetened chocolate after adding the condensed milk.

SULTANA CARAMELS

1 cup granulated sugar
½ cup milk
½ cup molasses
¼ cup butter or margarine
2 1-ounce squares unsweetened
    chocolate
1 teaspoon vanilla
½ cup broken California walnuts
½ cup light raisins

Butter sides of heavy 2-quart saucepan. In it combine sugar, milk, molasses, butter, and chocolate. Cook over low heat, stirring occasionally till smooth. Cook over medium heat to firm-ball stage (246°), stirring last few minutes to prevent sticking. Add vanilla. Place nuts and raisins in buttered 8x8x2-inch pan and pour caramel mixture over. Cool; cut in 1-inch squares. Makes about 1¼ pounds.

BROWN SUGAR NUT ROLL

  2 cups granulated sugar
  1 cup brown sugar
  1 cup evaporated milk
  ¼ cup corn syrup
  Dash salt
  1 cup chopped pecans

Butter sides of heavy 2-quart saucepan. In it combine sugars, milk, corn syrup, and salt. Stir over medium heat till sugars dissolve and mixture boils. Cook to soft-ball stage (236°) stirring frequently. Immediately remove from heat; cool to lukewarm (110°); *do not* stir.

Beat till fudge begins to hold its shape. Turn out on buttered surface. Knead fudge till it can be shaped, keeping hands well buttered.

Shape in two 7-inch rolls and roll immediately in chopped pecans, pressing nuts on to coat. Wrap in foil, clear plastic wrap, or waxed paper; chill till ready to slice. Cut in ½-inch slices. Makes about 28 pieces of candy.

Note: Mixture will curdle while cooking, but becomes smooth when you beat it.

FONDANT

  2 cups granulated sugar
  1½ cups boiling water
  ⅛ teaspoon cream of tartar *or*
    2 tablespoons light corn syrup

Butter sides of heavy 1½-quart saucepan. In it combine sugar, water, and cream of tartar or corn syrup. Stir over medium heat till sugar dissolves and mixture boils. Cook without stirring to soft-ball stage (238°). Immediately pour onto platter. *Do not* scrape pan.

Cool till fondant feels only slightly warm to the touch, about 30 minutes; do not move. Using spatula or wooden spoon, scrape fondant from edge of platter toward center, then work till creamy and stiff. Knead till smooth and free from lumps. Wrap; place in covered container to ripen 24 hours.

To tint and flavor fondant: For *vanilla* fondant, knead in 1 tablespoon soft butter and 1 teaspoon vanilla. For *pink peppermint* fondant, knead in 10 drops of peppermint extract and 4 drops red food coloring. Shape and decorate. Or, stuff dates, prunes, or figs with fondant and roll in confectioners' sugar.

MARZIPAN

Prepare 1 recipe Fondant and ripen 24 hours. Next day, warm fondant over hot water and work to a smooth cream (about 2 minutes), adding a few drops of water if needed. Work in one 8-ounce can (1 cup) almond paste till smooth. Place in bowl, cover with damp cloth, and let ripen several hours. Divide in parts; color with red, yellow, or green food coloring, and shape fruits (see below). Dry fruits overnight on their sides on waxed paper. Next day, add blushes or sugar coating.

Leaves: Tint some Marzipan green and form tiny leaves and berry "hulls." Or, use commercial leaves, if available.

Pears: Tint Marzipan yellow. Mold pear shape, using 2 teaspoons each. Add cloves for blossom ends and press on leaves. Next day, pat or brush on a pink blush, using red food coloring mixed with water.

Peaches: Tint Marzipan orange. Mold balls, using 1½ teaspoons each. Flatten on both ends. Crease one side with knife. Add clove at one end, leaves at the other. Next day, add pink blush, using food coloring.

Apples: Tint Marzipan green. Mold balls, using 1½ teaspoons each. Add clove at one end, leaves at other. Next day, add red blush, using red food coloring.

Bananas: Tint Marzipan yellow. Mold banana shapes, using 2 teaspoons each. Next day, tint ends green and streak with cocoa dissolved in equal amount of water.

Strawberries: Tint candy red. Roll in balls, using 1 teaspoon each. Shape point at one end and flatten the other. Add hull. Let dry overnight. Brush with corn syrup; roll in red sugar. Dry thoroughly.

SMALL MINTS

Cook 2 cups granulated sugar, ½ cup water, and ½ cup light corn syrup in 2-quart saucepan; stir till sugar dissolves. Cook to thread stage (232°) without stirring. Add ⅛ teaspoon cream of tartar; beat with wire whip till creamy. Flavor with few drops of flavored oils and tint with food coloring.

Drop from teaspoon onto waxed paper forming patties. (Keep pan over hot water while forming patties. Mixture hardens on cooling.) Store in tightly covered container. Makes 60.

Remarkable Fudge, Marzipan, Brown Sugar Nut Roll, Divinity, and Holiday Mints ring jewel box of Glazed Almonds. **Holiday Mints.** Combine one 3-ounce package cream cheese, 1 egg white, ¼ teaspoon peppermint extract, ¼ teaspoon salt, and 1 cup sifted confectioners' sugar. Gradually add 5½ to 5¾ cups additional confectioners' sugar; knead till smooth. Cover with damp cloth; let stand at room temperature 1 hour. For each candy roll, pat 2 tablespoons candy out to 6x1½-inch rectangle. Place one red or green gumdrop string on 1½-inch edge of rectangle. Roll up till candy covers gumdrop. Place a second gumdrop string on the rectangle and roll. Add third gumdrop string and complete candy roll, sealing ends. Roll gently to make candy round. Repeat with remaining candy. Makes about 5 dozen pieces.

So-good Southern pralines

Creamy-rich and filled with pecans, these luscious pralines are made in the tradition of the Old South. They're perfect for satisfying anyone's sweet tooth—family or guests.

Stir carefully to keep sugar crystals in lower part of pan. All crystals should be dissolved when candy boils. This helps to make it smooth.

When mixture starts to boil, it bubbles high in pan, so reduce heat and continue stirring with wooden spoon to keep it from boiling over.

SOUTHERN PRALINES

2 cups granulated sugar
¾ teaspoon soda
1 cup light cream
1½ tablespoons butter
2 cups pecan halves

Combine sugar and soda in 3-quart saucepan; mix well. Stir in cream. Bring to boiling over medium heat, stirring constantly. Cook and stir to soft-ball stage (234°). (Mixture caramelizes slightly as it cooks.) Remove from heat; add butter. Stir in pecans; beat till thick enough to drop from spoon (takes only 2 to 3 minutes). Drop from tablespoon on waxed paper. If candy becomes too stiff to drop, add a tablespoon of hot water. Makes 2½ dozen.

PRALINES

Butter sides of heavy 3-quart saucepan. In it combine 1½ cups brown sugar, 1½ cups granulated sugar, 3 tablespoons dark corn syrup, and 1 cup milk. Cook and stir over medium heat till sugars dissolve and mixture boils. Cook to soft-ball stage (234°), stirring occasionally. Cool 10 minutes. Add 1 teaspoon vanilla. Beat by hand 2 minutes. Add 1½ cups pecan halves; beat till mixture loses its gloss.

Drop by tablespoon onto waxed paper-lined cookie sheet. If candy becomes too stiff to drop, add a teaspoon of hot water. Makes 16.

RAISIN PRALINE CARAMELS

This candy leads a double life—it's chocolate coated caramels or raisin praline crunch—

1 cup raisins
¾ cup butter or margarine
1 cup brown sugar
½ cup semisweet chocolate pieces

Place raisins in buttered 8x8x2-inch baking pan. Combine butter and sugar in saucepan; cook and stir to hard-ball stage (254°). Pour over raisins. Top with chocolate pieces, spreading as they melt. Chill firm; cut in pieces.

Raisin Praline Crunch: Place raisins in buttered 13x9x2-inch pan. Cook butter and sugar to soft-crack stage (290°). Pour over raisins; top with *1 cup* chocolate pieces, spreading as they melt. Chill firm; break into pieces.

COFFEE CARAMELS

Line 9x5x3-inch pan with foil; butter lightly. In 2-quart saucepan, combine 1 cup granulated sugar, ½ cup brown sugar, ½ cup light corn syrup, 1½ cups light cream, 2 tablespoons instant coffee powder, and ¼ cup butter or margarine. Cook, stirring constantly, over low heat till sugars dissolve. Cook over medium heat, stirring occasionally, to firm-ball stage (248°). Remove from heat; stir in 1 teaspoon vanilla. Turn into prepared pan; cool. Cut in 36 pieces.

Remove pan from heat before adding butter and pecan halves. Measure butter accurately— too much may keep pralines from firming.

Candy drops easiest from a metal tablespoon. If necessary, add a tablespoon or so of hot water to keep candy at right stage for dropping.

Old-time Fudge

Fantastic fudge

OLD-TIME FUDGE

2 cups granulated sugar
¾ cup milk
2 1–ounce squares unsweetened
  chocolate
Dash salt
1 teaspoon light corn syrup
2 tablespoons butter or margarine
1 teaspoon vanilla

Butter sides of heavy 2-quart saucepan. In it combine first 5 ingredients. Stir over medium heat till sugar dissolves and mixture comes to boiling. Then cook to soft-ball stage (234°), stirring only if necessary.

Immediately remove pan from heat; add butter and cool to lukewarm (110°) without stirring. Add vanilla. Beat vigorously until fudge becomes very thick and starts to lose its gloss. Quickly spread in buttered shallow pan. Score while warm, cut when firm.

Note: If desired, quickly stir in ½ cup broken nuts at end of beating time.

Opera Fudge

Remarkable Fudge

SANTA'S FUDGE

Butter sides of a heavy 3-quart saucepan. In it combine 2 cups granulated sugar, ⅓ cup cocoa (regular-type, dry), dash salt, ⅔ cup water, and 2 tablespoons butter or margarine. Cook over medium heat, stirring constantly, till sugar dissolves and mixture comes to boiling. Cook to soft-ball stage (234°). Immediately remove pan from heat; cool to lukewarm (110°) without stirring. Add 1 teaspoon vanilla. Beat vigorously until fudge becomes very thick and starts to lose its gloss. Quickly stir in ½ cup broken California walnuts; spread in buttered 8x8x2-inch pan. Score in 1-inch squares while warm; cut fudge when firm.

Santa's Fudge

ROCKY ROAD

Not really a fudge, but the next best thing!

4 4½-ounce milk-chocolate bars
3 cups miniature marshmallows
¾ cup coarsely broken California walnuts

Partially melt chocolate bars over hot water; remove from heat and beat till smooth. Stir in marshmallows and nuts. Spread in buttered 8x8x2-inch pan. Chill. Cut when firm.

Penuche

Rocky Road

Perfect fudge? Here's how--

REMARKABLE FUDGE

Butter sides of a heavy 3-quart saucepan. In it combine 4 cups granulated sugar, one 14½-ounce can (1⅔ cups) evaporated milk, and 1 cup butter or margarine. Cook over medium heat to soft-ball stage (236°), stirring frequently. Remove from heat; add one 12-ounce package (2 cups) semisweet chocolate pieces, 1 pint marshmallow creme, 1 teaspoon vanilla, and 1 cup broken California walnuts. Beat till chocolate is melted and blended. Pour into buttered 13x9x2-inch pan. Score in squares while warm; cut when firm. Makes 4½ dozen 1½-inch pieces. If desired, top pieces with walnut halves.

1 Butter sides of a heavy, high-sided saucepan, top to bottom. Then, when fudge bubbles up, grains of sugar can't cling and unwanted crystals won't form.

2 Stir fudge till it comes to boiling and *all* the grains of sugar are dissolved. Sugar will dissolve easily at this stage but can't after mixture concentrates. One sugar crystal can start a chain reaction and make the entire batch of fudge grainy! Wait to clip on candy thermometer till the mixture boils.

3 Check temperature of fudge often after it reaches 220°—it'll climb fast after this point. The best way is to use a candy thermometer. Some people like to double check stages with the cold water test, too!

4 After candy has cooled *undisturbed* to 110° (bottom of pan should feel comfortably warm to your hand), add extract and start beating vigorously. Don't stop beating too soon— and no resting! Get help if necessary.

5 Pour fudge at just the right moment— fudge will seem to stiffen and lose its gloss. This is also the time to add chopped nuts. *Push* mixture from pan with rubber spatula—*don't scrape* around sides.

6 Score fudge while warm for neater squares, using tip of knife. Dip knife in water when necessary. Now's the time to press a perfect nut half on each square. When candy is cool and firm, cut along score marks.

OPERA FUDGE

It's blond fudge at its best!

2 cups granulated sugar
½ cup milk
½ cup light cream
1 tablespoon light corn syrup
½ teaspoon salt
. . .
1 tablespoon butter or margarine
1 teaspoon vanilla
¼ cup chopped candied cherries

Butter sides of a heavy 2-quart saucepan. In it combine sugar, milk, cream, corn syrup, and salt. Cook over medium heat, stirring constantly till sugar dissolves and mixture comes to boiling. Then cook to soft-ball stage (238°). Immediately remove from heat and cool to lukewarm (110°) without stirring. Add butter and vanilla. Beat vigorously until mixture becomes very thick and starts to lose its gloss. Quickly stir in the chopped cherries and spread in a buttered 9x5x3-inch pan. Score in squares while warm; cut when cool and firm.

PENUCHE

Rich and creamy brown-sugar fudge. A favorite of grandmothers (granddads, too!)—

1½ cups granulated sugar
1 cup brown sugar
⅓ cup light cream
⅓ cup milk
2 tablespoons butter or margarine
. . .
1 teaspoon vanilla
½ cup broken pecans

Butter sides of heavy 2-quart saucepan. In it combine sugars, cream, milk, and butter. Cook over medium heat, stirring constantly, till sugars dissolve and mixture comes to boiling. Then cook to soft-ball stage (238°), stirring only if necessary. Immediately remove from heat and cool to lukewarm (110°) without stirring. Add vanilla. Beat vigorously till fudge becomes very thick and starts to lose its gloss. Quickly stir in nuts and spread in buttered shallow pan or small platter. Score in squares while warm; cut when cool and firm.

PEANUT-BUTTER FUDGE

Creamy smooth with bits of crunchy peanuts. There's a bonus with this candy—no hard beating required—

2 cups granulated sugar
⅔ cup milk
½ of pint jar marshmallow creme
1 cup chunk-style peanut butter
1 6-ounce package (1 cup) semisweet chocolate pieces
1 teaspoon vanilla

Butter sides of heavy 2-quart saucepan. In it combine sugar and milk. Stir over medium heat till sugar dissolves and mixture boils. Cook to soft-ball stage (234°). Remove from heat; quickly add marshmallow creme, peanut butter, chocolate, and vanilla; stir just till blended. Pour into buttered 9x9x2-inch pan. Score 1-inch squares while warm; cut when firm.

COFFEE DOT FUDGE

Mocha-flavored candy with chocolate and nuts—

3 cups granulated sugar
1 cup milk
½ cup light cream
2 tablespoons instant coffee powder
1 tablespoon light corn syrup
Dash salt
3 tablespoons butter or margarine
1 teaspoon vanilla
½ 6-ounce package (½ cup) semisweet
   chocolate pieces
½ cup broken pecans

Butter sides of heavy 3-quart saucepan. In it combine sugar, milk, cream, instant coffee, corn syrup, and salt. Heat over medium heat, stirring constantly, till sugar dissolves and mixture comes to boiling. Cook to soft-ball stage (234°), stirring only if necessary. Immediately remove from heat; add butter and cool to lukewarm (110°) without stirring. Add·vanilla. Beat vigorously till fudge becomes very thick and starts to lose its gloss. At once stir in chocolate pieces and pecans. Quickly spread in buttered shallow pan or small platter. Score in squares while warm; top each square with pecan half. Cut when firm.

CARAMEL FUDGE

A jar of sundae sauce adds flavor in a hurry—

2 cups granulated sugar
1 6-ounce can (⅔ cup) evaporated milk
2 tablespoons light corn syrup
1 10-ounce jar vanilla caramel sauce
1 teaspoon vanilla
¼ teaspoon maple flavoring
½ cup chopped California walnuts

Butter sides of heavy 2-quart saucepan. In it combine sugar, milk, syrup, and caramel sauce. Stir over medium heat till sugar dissolves and mixture comes to boiling. Cook to soft-ball stage (235°), stirring occasionally. Remove from heat. Stir in vanilla and maple flavoring; beat just till mixture begins to lose its gloss. Stir in nuts. Pour into buttered 8x8x2-inch pan. Score into 1½-inch squares while warm; cut when firm.

DOUBLE-LAYER FUDGE

Like eating two kinds of candy in one—

4½ cups granulated sugar
1 1-pint jar marshmallow creme
2 6-ounce cans (1⅓ cups)
   evaporated milk
½ cup butter or margarine
Dash salt
. . .
1 6-ounce package (1 cup) semisweet chocolate pieces
1 5½-ounce package (about 1 cup)
   peanut butter pieces

Combine sugar, marshmallow creme, evaporated milk, butter, and salt in a 3-quart saucepan. Cook over medium heat, stirring constantly, till mixture boils. Boil gently, stirring frequently, for 5 minutes. Divide mixture in half. To one half (about 3 cups) stir in chocolate pieces till melted and blended. Pour into buttered 13x9x2-inch pan. To remaining half of mixture, add the peanut butter pieces, beating till smooth.* Pour over chocolate layer. Cool. Cut candy into 1-inch squares.

*You may have to beat mixture with rotary beater at this point till all peanut butter pieces are melted and mixture is smooth.

Divinity that's divine

Perfect Divinity. In 2-quart saucepan, combine 2½ cups granulated sugar, ½ cup light corn syrup, ½ cup water, and ¼ teaspoon salt. Cook to hard-ball stage (260°), stirring only till sugar dissolves. Meanwhile, as temperature of syrup reaches 250°, beat 2 egg whites till stiff peaks form. When syrup reaches 260°, very gradually add the syrup to egg whites, beating at high speed on electric mixer.

Add 1 teaspoon vanilla and beat till candy holds its shape (about 4 to 5 minutes). If desired, add ½ cup chopped nuts. Drop from a teaspoon onto waxed paper; swirl top. Makes 40.

PARTY PINK DIVINITY

 3 cups granulated sugar
 ¾ cup light corn syrup
 ¾ cup water
 ¼ teaspoon salt
 2 egg whites
 ½ 3-ounce package cherry-flavored
    gelatin
 1 teaspoon vanilla
 1 cup chopped nuts
 ¾ cup flaked coconut, tinted pink*

Combine sugar, corn syrup, water, and salt in buttered heavy 2-quart saucepan. Cook over medium heat, stirring constantly, till mixture boils. Then cook without stirring to hard-ball stage (250°). Remove from heat.

Beat egg whites in large bowl of mixer till soft peaks form. Gradually add gelatin, beating till stiff peaks form. Slowly pour in syrup, beating constantly at high speed. Continue beating till mixture begins to lose its gloss. Stir in chopped nuts. Drop from teaspoon onto waxed paper or into small paper muffin liners. Sprinkle with tinted coconut. Makes about 2 pounds or 4 dozen medium-sized pieces of candy.

*Place coconut in glass jar. Add few drops food coloring; cover and shake till colored.

SEA FOAM

Butter sides of heavy 1½-quart saucepan. In it combine 1½ cups brown sugar, ½ cup granulated sugar, ½ cup hot water, ¼ cup light corn syrup, and ¼ teaspoon salt. Cook, stirring constantly, till sugar dissolves and mixture comes to boiling. Then cook to hard-ball stage (250°) without stirring. Remove pan from heat.

Immediately beat 2 egg whites till stiff. Pour hot syrup in a thin stream over beaten egg whites, beating constantly at high speed on electric mixer. Add 1 teaspoon vanilla. Continue beating till mixture forms soft peaks and begins to lose gloss, about 10 minutes.

Stir in ½ cup broken pecans, if desired. Drop from teaspoon onto waxed paper, swirling each candy to a peak. Makes 1 pound.

Hard-crackin' candies

ORANGE COCONUT BRITTLE

2¼ cups granulated sugar
¼ cup light corn syrup
1 teaspoon shredded orange peel
½ cup orange juice
2 tablespoons butter or margarine
1 3½-ounce can (1⅓ cups)
  flaked coconut

Butter sides of heavy 3-quart saucepan. In it combine sugar, corn syrup, peel, and orange juice. Cook over medium heat to hard-crack stage (300°), stirring occasionally. Remove from heat; stir in butter. Pour in thin layer into buttered 15½x10½x1-inch pan or large platter. Sprinkle coconut over it evenly. When cold, crack. Makes about 1¼ pounds.

LOLLIPOP CLOWNS

3 cups granulated sugar
¾ cup light corn syrup
3 tablespoons vinegar
⅓ cup boiling water
¼ cup butter or margarine
Dash salt
Wooden skewers
Fruit-flavored hard-candy circles

Combine sugar, corn syrup, vinegar, and water; stir till sugar dissolves. Cook to hard-crack stage (300°). Remove from heat; add butter and salt. Cool until mixture thickens slightly. Quickly drop from tablespoon over skewers placed 5 inches apart on greased cookie sheet to form 3-inch lollipops. Make faces with the candy circles. Makes about 16.

A gleaming, translucent thread of orange syrup curls down onto a polished marble slab. When cool, it makes a crunchy brittle candy. Orange Coconut Brittle tastes as refreshing as the tantalizing citrus scent of the syrup. Tiny flecks of orange peel add extra zest and flaked coconut forms the snowy white crown.

ALMOND BUTTER CRUNCH

1 cup butter or margarine
1⅓ cups granulated sugar
1 tablespoon light corn syrup
3 tablespoons water
1 cup *coarsely* chopped almonds,
  toasted
4 4½-ounce milk chocolate bars,
  melted
1 cup *finely* chopped almonds,
  toasted

In large saucepan melt butter; add sugar, corn syrup, and water. Cook, stirring occasionally, to hard-crack stage (300°).* Quickly stir in *coarsely* chopped nuts; spread in ungreased 13x9x2-inch pan. Cool thoroughly. Turn out on waxed paper; spread top with *half* the chocolate; sprinkle with *half* the finely chopped nuts. Cover with waxed paper; invert. Spread with chocolate; sprinkle remaining nuts atop. If necessary, chill to firm; crack in pieces.

*Watch carefully after 280°.

JEWEL CANDIES

1 cup granulated sugar
½ cup light corn syrup
⅓ cup water
¼ teaspoon flavoring oil
Food coloring

Line 8x8x2-inch pan with foil, extending foil up sides; butter foil. Butter sides of 1-quart saucepan. In it combine sugar, syrup, and water. Bring to boiling, stirring constantly till sugar is dissolved. Cook to hard-crack stage (300°). Remove from heat; add desired flavoring and coloring. Pour into prepared pan.

When just beginning to set around the edges, lift foil out of pan (candy will still be runny and hot in center). With scissors, cut candy into 1-inch strips, beginning with outside edges. Then cut into very small pieces of irregular shape. To work fast enough, this requires 2 or 3 people to cut. Make only one batch at a time. Makes ½ pound.

BUTTERY PEANUT BRITTLE

2 cups granulated sugar
1 cup light corn syrup
½ cup water
1 cup butter or margarine
2 cups raw or roasted peanuts
1 teaspoon soda

Combine sugar, corn syrup, and water in 3-quart saucepan. Cook and stir till sugar dissolves. When syrup boils, blend in butter. Stir frequently after mixture reaches the syrup stage (230°). Add nuts when the temperature reaches soft-crack stage (280°) and stir constantly till temperature reaches the hard-crack stage (305°). Remove from heat. Quickly stir in soda, mixing thoroughly. Pour onto two cookie sheets or two 15½x10½x1-inch pans.

As the candy cools, stretch it out thin by lifting and pulling from edges, using two forks. Loosen from pans as soon as possible; turn candy over. Break in pieces. Makes 2½ pounds.

CRYSTAL-CUT CANDIES

Color one batch red, do another one green—

Combine 2 cups granulated sugar, ½ cup light corn syrup, ½ cup water, and dash salt. Bring to boiling. Cook to soft-crack stage (290°). Add few drops red *or* green food coloring and 4 to 6 drops oil of cinnamon *or* oil of wintergreen; gently swirl mixture to blend. (Use red coloring with cinnamon, green coloring with wintergreen.) Pour into 8x8x2-inch metal pan. Let stand few minutes till film forms over top.

Mark candy in little puffs, each about ¾-inch square. Because candy is cooler at edges, start marking from outside and work toward the center. Using a broad spatula or pancake turner, press a line across pan ¾ inch from edge, *being careful not to break through the film on surface.* Repeat around other 3 sides of pan, intersecting lines at corners to form squares. (If lines do not hold shape, candy is not cool enough.) Continue marking lines to center.

While waiting for center to cool enough, retrace previous lines, pressing the spatula deeper *but not breaking film.* When spatula may be pressed to bottom of pan in all lines, candy will be shaped in square puffs. Cool, then turn out and break into pieces. Makes 100.

MOLASSES TAFFY

Don't miss the fun of an old-fashioned taffy party! Pull till the candy is golden-blond—

2 cups granulated sugar
1 cup light molasses
¼ cup water
2 teaspoons vinegar
2 tablespoons butter or margarine
½ teaspoon soda

Butter sides of heavy 2-quart saucepan. In it combine sugar, molasses, and water. Cook slowly, stirring constantly, till sugar dissolves. Then bring to boiling; add vinegar and cook to soft-crack stage (270°). Remove from heat; add butter and sift in soda; stir to mix.

Turn out (don't scrape pan) on buttered platter or large shallow pan. For even cooling, use spatula to turn edges to center. Pull the taffy while as warm as you can handle; use only fingertips to pull—butter hands so candy won't stick. When candy is light taffy color and hard to pull, cut in fourths and pull each piece into a long strand, ½ inch thick. With buttered scissors, quickly snip in bite-size pieces. Wrap each piece in clear plastic wrap.

SALT WATER TAFFY

2 cups granulated sugar
1 cup light corn syrup
1½ cups water
1½ teaspoons salt
2 tablespoons butter or margarine
¼ teaspoon oil of peppermint
7 drops green food coloring

Combine sugar, syrup, water, and salt in 2-quart saucepan. Cook slowly, stirring constantly, till sugar is dissolved. Continue to cook to hard-ball stage (260°) without stirring.

Remove from heat; stir in butter, flavoring, and food coloring. Pour into buttered 15½x10½x1-inch pan. Cool until comfortable to handle. Butter hands; gather taffy into a ball and pull. When candy is light color and gets hard to pull, cut in fourths; pull each piece into long strand about ½ inch thick.

With buttered scissors, quickly snip taffy in bite-size pieces. Wrap each piece in clear plastic wrap. Makes 1¼ pounds of candy.

Crunchy candied apples

Crisp apples and a chewy coating of melted caramels make a perfect ending to a festive fall buffet.

CARAMEL APPLES

Melt one 14-ounce package (about 50) vanilla caramels with 2 tablespoons water in top of double boiler, stirring frequently till mixture is smooth. Add dash salt.

Stick wooden skewer into blossom end of 6 unpared crisp medium apples. Dip apples in caramel syrup and turn until bottom half of apples are completely coated. (If syrup is too stiff, add few drops water).

At once roll bottoms of coated apples in chopped California walnuts. Set on cookie sheet covered with waxed paper. Chill till the caramel coating is firm. Top sticks with large pieces of corn candy, if desired.

CINNAMON APPLES

Munching these will keep the kiddies busy— and happy—quite a while! The red candy coating is sparkling clear—

8 crisp, medium apples
8 wooden skewers
. . .
4 cups granulated sugar
1⅓ cups light corn syrup
2 cups water
Dash salt
1¼ teaspoons red food coloring
. . .
10 drops oil of cinnamon

Wash and dry the apples; remove stems. Stick skewer into stem end of each apple. Butter sides of heavy saucepan. In saucepan, combine sugar, corn syrup, water, salt, and food coloring. Cook, stirring constantly, till sugar dissolves and mixture comes to boiling. Continue cooking, without stirring, till mixture reaches the hard-crack stage (300°).

Remove from heat; quickly stir in the oil of cinnamon. Turn each apple in syrup to coat (tilt pan, so syrup is deep enough to cover). Twirl apple to spread coating evenly—let the excess syrup drip back into pan. Set apples on buttered cookie sheet. Chill till firm.

Note: If desired, make lollipops to use the remaining syrup. Arrange wooden skewers 4 inches apart on buttered cookie sheet. Drop hot syrup from tip of tablespoon over the skewers to form 2- or 3-inch candy suckers.

Pastel Popcorn Christmas Tree makes a delectable holiday decoration. Colorful "branches" are made of plump popcorn balls, some pink peppermint, some vanilla. "Marshmallow Sparkles" sport pink coats and real berry-patch flavor. Top tree with a red bow and candy canes.

POPCORN PERSONALITIES

Great idea for a rainy day or children's party—

Begin the fun by all making popcorn balls. Pick a theme for the popcorn characters— favorite storybook folk, holiday symbols, or animal zoo. Skewer balls into big apples.

Make Marshmallow Stickum: Melt $\frac{2}{3}$ cup miniature marshmallows (or 6 big ones) with 2 teaspoons shortening over low heat. While warm, dip assorted candies into stickum; then anchor on balls to make characters' features.

PASTEL POPCORN TREE

White Popcorn Balls

5 quarts popped corn (about 2 cups unpopped)
2 cups granulated sugar
1½ cups water
½ teaspoon salt
½ cup light corn syrup
1 teaspoon vinegar
1 teaspoon vanilla

Keep popcorn hot and crisp in slow oven (300° to 325°). Butter sides of saucepan. In it, combine granulated sugar, water, salt, syrup, and vinegar. Cook to hard-ball stage (250°). Stir in vanilla. Pour cooked syrup slowly over hot popped corn, stirring just enough to combine thoroughly. Butter hands lightly and shape popcorn mixture into 2-inch balls.

Pink Popcorn Balls

Prepare as for white popcorn balls above but omit vinegar (to insure pretty pink color), and vanilla. Add ¼ teaspoon red food coloring and ¼ teaspoon peppermint extract to cooked syrup. Shape some of the red popcorn mixture into eleven balls 2½ inches in diameter, the remainder into 2-inch balls.

Marshmallow Sparkles

Red food coloring
Strawberry- or raspberry-flavored gelatin (½ of 3-ounce package)
Marshmallows, large and miniature

Add food coloring, a few drops at a time, to gelatin, mixing well to obtain desired color. (A blender does the trick beautifully.) Dip a few marshmallows by hand into water. Drain excess moisture by shaking in paper toweling. Roll marshmallows in colored gelatin and allow to dry thoroughly.

To assemble tree: On flat plate or tray, arrange a circle of the eleven 2½-inch pink balls, securing one to the other with toothpicks. Fill in center with 7 white balls. Pyramid remaining balls, alternating colors; continue to fill in centers with white balls. If desired, omit top ball and carefully insert 3 large candy canes tied with a red bow. Tuck in Marshmallow Sparkles.

Popcorn tricks

CARAMEL POPCORN BALLS

4 tablespoons butter or margarine
1 cup brown sugar
½ cup light corn syrup
½ 15-ounce can (⅔ cup) sweetened
   condensed milk
½ teaspoon vanilla
5 quarts popped corn

In saucepan, combine butter, brown sugar, and corn syrup. Stir well and bring to boiling over medium heat. Stir in milk; simmer, stirring constantly, till mixture cooks to soft-ball stage (234° to 238°). Stir in vanilla.

Pour syrup over popped corn and stir well till kernels are coated. Butter hands lightly; shape coated popcorn into balls about 3½ inches in diameter. Makes about 15 balls.

CINNAMON POPCORN BALLS

Keep 3 quarts popped corn hot and crisp in slow oven (300° to 325°). Butter sides of saucepan. In it combine 1 cup granulated sugar, ⅓ cup red cinnamon candies, ⅔ cup water, 1 tablespoon vinegar, and ¼ teaspoon salt. Cook to hard-ball stage (250°), stirring till sugar dissolves. Add 1 or 2 drops oil of cinnamon, if desired. Pour slowly over hot popped corn, mixing well to coat every kernel. Butter hands. Press coated popcorn lightly into balls, 1½ inches in diameter. Makes about 3 dozen small balls.

QUICK CARAMEL POPCORN

2 quarts popped corn
½ pound (28) vanilla caramels
2 tablespoons water

Keep popped corn hot and crisp in slow oven (300° to 325°). Combine caramels and 2 tablespoons water in top of double boiler; melt over water, stirring frequently. Add dash salt. Place popped corn in large bowl and pour sauce over; toss till corn is well coated. Butter hands and lightly shape in balls, 1½ inches in diameter.

BEST-EVER CANDY CORN

Tastes almost like a popcorn brittle—

2½ quarts popped corn
1 pound (2¼ cups) brown sugar
½ cup light corn syrup
½ cup water
½ cup butter or margarine
2 teaspoons salt
1 tablespoon vanilla
1 cup salted peanuts

Keep popped corn crisp in slow oven (300° to 325°). In large saucepan, combine sugar, syrup, water, butter, and salt. Cook over moderate heat, stirring occasionally, until syrup reaches soft-crack stage (290°). Remove from heat; stir in 1 tablespoon vanilla.

In large buttered bowl or pan, mix nuts and popcorn. Pour syrup in fine stream over mixture. Working quickly, mix well until kernels are completely coated. Spread out thin on buttered cookie sheets or platters. Quickly separate into bite-size clusters with 2 buttered forks. Cool. Makes about 3½ quarts.

POPCORN POPS

Shape popcorn in paper cups; add skewers for easy handling—

4 quarts popped corn (⅔ cup
   unpopped)
1 cup peanuts
1 cup light molasses
1 cup granulated sugar
1 teaspoon salt

Combine popped corn and peanuts in large bowl or pan. In 2-quart saucepan, combine molasses, sugar, and salt; cook over medium heat to hard-ball stage (260°). Pour hot syrup slowly over popped corn, stirring till mixture is well coated. Press popcorn mixture into 5-ounce cold-drink cups. Insert a wooden skewer in each; let cool. Push on bottom of cup to remove popcorn pops. Makes 16 or 17 pops. Paper doilies add a gay touch.

Nut and fruit confections

Candied Grapefruit Peel with a bright new and tasty twist! Pretty colors and added fruit flavor come from strawberry-, lemon-, or lime-flavored gelatin. For extra fancy peels, use cookie cutters to make heart, shamrock, or other appropriate shapes; then roll in giant-size sugar crystals or matching colored sugar. Peels double as decorations in clear jars.

CANDIED GRAPEFRUIT PEEL

2 medium grapefruit
1½ cups granulated sugar
¾ cups water
¼ teaspoon salt

. . .

1 3-ounce package lemon-, lime-, or strawberry-flavored gelatin

Score grapefruit peel in 4 lengthwise sections with point of knife. Loosen from pulp with bowl of spoon. Remove most of the white membrane from peel. Cut peel into ¼-inch strips or various shapes with cookie cutters.

Place 2 cups of cut peel in large pan. Cover generously with cold water. Boil 20 minutes. Drain. Repeat process twice with fresh water each time. Drain thoroughly.

Combine sugar, water, and salt in 2-quart saucepan. Cook and stir to dissolve sugar. Add peel; bring to boil. Simmer 20 minutes or till peel is just translucent. Gradually add gelatin, stirring over low heat till gelatin is dissolved.

Remove peel from syrup; drain on rack. Let stand 20 minutes. Roll each piece in granulated or colored sugar. Let dry on rack several hours or overnight. Store in covered jar.

CANDIED TANGERINE PEEL

8 medium tangerines (or 3 medium oranges)
4 cups cold water
1 tablespoon salt

. . .

2 cups granulated sugar
½ cup water

Cut peel of each tangerine in fourths; loosen from pulp with bowl of spoon. Add salt to the 4 cups water; add peel. Weight with a plate to keep peel under water. Let stand overnight.

Drain; wash thoroughly. Cover with cold water; heat to boiling. Drain. Repeat 3 times. This helps remove the bitter taste.

With kitchen scissors, cut peel in strips. In saucepan, combine 2 cups cut peel, sugar, and the ½ cup water. Cook and stir till sugar dissolves. Cook slowly till peel is translucent. Drain thoroughly; roll in granulated sugar. Dry on rack. Store in covered container.

STUFFED DATES

4½ cups sifted confectioners' sugar
⅔ cup sweetened condensed milk
¼ teaspoon salt
1½ teaspoons vanilla
¼ teaspoon almond extract
1½ pounds whole pitted dates

Gradually add *4 cups* of the sugar to milk, blending well. Mix in salt, vanilla, and almond extract. Sprinkle remaining ½ cup sugar on a board and knead fondant till smooth and creamy, working in the sugar. Wrap in foil. Place in the refrigerator to ripen for 24 hours.

Stuff dates with fondant. Garnish each with walnut halves, bits of candied cherries, or flaked coconut if desired. Recipe makes enough fondant to stuff 9 to 10 dozen dates.

FRUIT BALLS

1½ cups prunes, cooked and pitted
1½ cups pitted dates
¾ cup dried apricots
½ cup raisins
1 cup California walnuts
¼ cup sugar
¼ cup concentrated orange juice, thawed
1 3½-ounce can (1⅓ cups) flaked coconut

Grind prunes, dates, apricots, raisins, and walnuts with coarse blade of a food grinder. Add sugar and orange juice. Form into 1-inch balls; roll in coconut. Makes 10 dozen.

CHOCOLATE CHERRIES

Drain one 8-ounce jar whole maraschino cherries thoroughly on paper towels. Prepare one 12-ounce package chocolate fudge mix according to package directions, except leave mixture over simmering water after it becomes glossy. Using fork, dip each cherry into fudge mixture, turning to coat evenly. Push onto waxed paper with another fork. Stir fudge mixture frequently. Pour remaining fudge into a small buttered pan. Makes 2½ dozen.

Note: These will not freeze or store well.

SPICY WALNUTS

2½ cups California walnut halves
1 cup granulated sugar
½ cup water
1 teaspoon cinnamon
½ teaspoon salt
1½ teaspoons vanilla

Heat walnut halves at 375° for 5 minutes, stirring once. Butter sides of heavy 2-quart saucepan. In it combine sugar, water, cinnamon, and salt. Cook and stir till sugar dissolves and mixture boils. Cook, without stirring, to soft-ball stage (236°). Remove from heat.

Beat by hand 1 minute or till mixture just begins to get creamy. Add vanilla and warm nuts; stir gently till nuts are well-coated and mixture is creamy. Turn out on buttered platter or cookie sheet. Separate at once, using two forks. Makes about 1 pound.

SWEDISH NUTS

½ pound (1½ cups) almonds
½ pound (2 cups) California
   walnut halves
2 egg whites
1 cup granulated sugar
½ cup butter or margarine

Toast almonds and walnuts in slow oven (325°) till light brown. Beat egg whites and dash salt till soft mounds form; gradually add sugar and beat to stiff peaks. Fold nuts into meringue. Melt butter in 15½x10½x1-inch pan; spread nut mixture over butter. Bake at 325° about 30 minutes, stirring every 10 minutes, or till nuts are coated with a brown covering and no butter remains in pan. Cool. Makes 5 to 6 cups.

COFFEE WALNUTS

Combine 1 cup brown sugar, ½ cup granulated sugar, ½ cup dairy sour cream, and 1 tablespoon instant coffee powder in saucepan. Cook and stir to soft-ball stage (236°). Remove from heat; stir in 1 teaspoon vanilla. Add 3 cups California walnut halves, stirring gently till all are coated. Arrange in single layer on buttered cookie sheet. Separate nuts with forks or let dry; break in pieces. Makes 4 cups.

Glazed Almonds—a little sweet, a little salty, with wonderful butter flavor. Easy as 1-2-3!

Glazed Almonds: Combine 1 cup whole almonds, ½ cup granulated sugar, and 2 tablespoons butter or margarine in heavy skillet. Cook, over medium heat, stirring constantly, till almonds are toasted and sugar is golden brown, about 15 minutes. Stir in ½ teaspoon vanilla. Spread nuts on sheet of aluminum foil. Sprinkle lightly with salt. Cool; then break into 2- or 3-nut clusters with forks.

CARAMEL NUTS

1 cup brown sugar
½ cup granulated sugar
½ cup light cream
2 tablespoons light corn syrup
1 tablespoon butter or margarine
1 tablespoon vanilla
2 cups California walnut halves

Combine sugars, cream, and corn syrup in a 1½-quart saucepan; cook to soft-ball stage (236°). Add butter and vanilla. Remove from heat and cool to lukewarm (110°) without stirring. Beat just until mixture begins to lose its gloss; add nuts and stir till well coated. Turn out on waxed paper; separate nuts with two forks. Makes about 4 cups nut confection.

INDEX

Additional recipes

Pages of this final section are for adding recipes from future issues of Better Homes and Gardens magazine and other favorite cookies and candies recipes.